UNRAVELED

A MOTHER AND SON STORY OF ADDICTION AND REDEMPTION

LAURA COOK BOLDT
& TOM H. BOLDT

This book is a memoir reflecting the authors' present recollections of experiences over time. Its story and its words are the authors' alone. Some details and characteristics may be changed, some events may be compressed, and some dialogue may be recreated. Some names and identifying characteristics of persons referenced in this book, as well as identifying places, have been changed to protect the privacy of the individuals and their families.

Published by River Grove Books
Austin, TX
www.rivergrovebooks.com

Distributed by River Grove Books

"Beatitudes for the Weird" by Jacob Nordby reproduced by kind permission of the author.
Design and composition by Greenleaf Book Group
Cover design by Greenleaf Book Group
Cover photo by Mae Mu on Unsplash.com

Publisher's Cataloging-in-Publication data is available.

Print ISBN: 978-1-63299-319-9

eBook ISBN: 978-1-63299-320-5

First Edition

Donohue

PRAISE FOR *UNRAVELED*

"*Unraveled* is a unique, heartfelt, and gripping mother–son story of the power of accountability, healing, faith, hope, and redemption. This is a raw and honest look into their mutual journeys from active alcohol and drug addiction into recovery. The courage and painstaking experiences are riveting and invite readers to witness their profound path to sobriety. Parents and friends of someone who is either in treatment or needs to be in treatment—and addicts in recovery along with their families—will find this story life changing."

–TIM RYAN, Activist, Speaker, TV Personality, Thought Leader, TEDx Speaker, and Author of *From Dope to Hope: A Man in Recovery*

"*Unraveled* is not just another book about the use of drugs and alcohol leading to recovery. This is the story of lives stitched together with the hread of redemption, new beginnings, new thoughts, ideas, and perspecves. It is one of courage, adaptability, and determination. The authors, oth mother and son, skillfully and honestly weave together a tapestry inner strength, familial dedication, and empowerment. Both stories mplement one another as they together meld a sometimes comical sometimes tragic human experience. Their family system embodies ngth, courage, integrity, and character. This is a must-read for those ing for hope through difficult times of addiction and recovery."

–NORFLEET H. RAND, MSW, LCSW, Relationship, Family, and Individual Counselor, St. Louis, Missouri

"I'm convinced this outstanding book will help many. I've worked with several thousand people in recovery over my 33-year career and established and worked with numerous addiction treatment programs in this country and abroad. This is a story of a courageous and outstanding young man, and it will inspire those of us who are in and out of the field of addiction recovery to want to help in whatever way we can."

—**LARRY PEDERSON,** Founder of the first residential Department of Defense treatment program, Consultant for local addiction programs, and Volunteer for jail ministry, Durango, Colorado

In loving memory of
Mary Margaret Blair — "Mom"/ "Granny"
Thank you for leading the way with grace.

Thomas Henry Boldt — "Pop"
An authentic example of a life well lived.

• • •

In honor of
TMB-WEB-PWB-WMB
Aka: Tribe Solid

• • •

With a sober toast to Faith, Gratitude,
genuine laughter, and all of their healing powers.

• • •

A giant shout-out to our extended family, dear
friends, those who helped us in our mutual
journeys, and to our amazing friends of Bill W.

• • •

Last but not least—for those who still suffer.

Beatitudes for the Weird

Blessed are the weird people
—poets, misfits, writers, mystics,
heretics, painters & troubadours—
for they teach us to see the world through different eyes.
Blessed are those who embrace the intensity of life's
pain and pleasure,
for they shall be rewarded with uncommon ecstasy.
Blessed are ye who see beauty in ugliness,
for you shall transform our vision of how the
world might be.
Blessed are the bold and whimsical,
for their imagination shatters ancient boundaries
of fear for us all.
Blessed are ye who are mocked for unbridled expression
of love in all its forms,
because your kind of crazy is exactly that freedom
For which the world is unconsciously begging.
Blessed are those who have endured breaking by life,
for they are the resplendent cracks through
which the light shines.

—Jacob Nordby

PROLOGUE

TOMMY—

Before I started writing all of this down, I had to do some serious thinking. There are already a ton of books out there that deal with addiction and recovery. Some of them are pretty good. Intense. Hopeful. Others, not so much. A few have been made into some pretty cool movies, too: *Trainspotting. Requiem for a Dream.* That movie *Flight*, where Denzel Washington plays a pilot who is a major addict. Functioning, but still—this guy shouldn't have been at the controls of an Xbox, never mind a 747 full of people.

And more recently, you have that Steve Carell movie, *Beautiful Boy*. The list goes on, and for good reason. Hollywood loves this shit, the way they love stories about the mentally handicapped. Maybe it's the spectacle of watching someone struggle to overcome impossible odds on their way to redemption—like that old saying, *If it doesn't kill you, it makes you stronger.*

Or maybe it's something else.

Maybe it's the actors. They love playing these roles, and it's no small secret why. It gives them the chance to behave like an unhinged maniac, staggering through the night, baying at the moon, generally destroying shit like personal property and the lives of others. If they go for the whole method acting thing, they're probably really getting wasted or high, all in the name of research.

I can see it now: a famous actor leaning out of his car window, squinting into the beam of a flashlight, slurring his words: "Officer, there's no need for me to step from the car. I'm a professional actor. Highly trained. This is all part of my research. Preparing for a role."

And the guy slumped in the seat next to him?

"Total amateur. A lightweight. Nowhere near my level. Can't even hold his appletini."

I wonder if that works when you're famous. While I'm no actor, I do know cops can be a little touchy when they realize you're driving under the influence.

When your mind is warped with drugs and alcohol, you tend to rationalize the craziest shit. Everyday normal stuff doesn't seem to register. You're even surprised when the cop points out that you've been driving over your neighbors' lawns instead of staying on the road.

How the fuck did that happen?

You get the picture—hypothetically speaking. But for me, it's not hypothetical. Sadly, driving under the influence is something I can relate to.

Still, I don't see Hollywood knocking on my door anytime soon. Unless it's Netflix looking for those DVDs I never returned.

But I digress.

Where was I? Oh, yeah. You know—that old saying that kind of sounds like some preachy bullshit unless you actually live it yourself.

If it doesn't kill you, it makes you stronger.

I know. Total cliché, right? But there's truth in it. Addiction is a serious ailment. It affects a lot of people in this country—more than most of us realize. Just look at the so-called *opioid epidemic.* It's out there, and it's a very real threat—whether or not you know it yet.

According to the US government's Health Resources and Services Administration, 166 people die every day from opioid-related drug overdoses. To put it in perspective, that's even more than the number of people who are killed by extreme violence each day.

One hundred sixty-six people, every single day.

That's a staggering body count, and it's gotten politicians talking. Unfortunately, all of this talk isn't really getting us anywhere; it takes so much more. There's still not enough actually happening to make things better.

A lot of gifted people have struggled with addiction. Many people I admired sadly lost this struggle. The fatalities are off the charts.

Look at the number of amazing musicians, with all the talent in the world, dead from addiction. Whatever demon they were fighting, it won. It got the best of them. And I'm not talking some one-and-done, video game smackdown. I'm talking about a slow and agonizing battle where the winner takes all. There's nothing sexy about that kind of journey.

The list is long and heartbreaking. It happens so much, they could dedicate an entire wing of the Rock and Roll Hall of Fame to these guys: Janis Joplin. Jim Morrison. Jimi Hendrix. Keith Moon. Sid Vicious. Kurt Cobain. And more recently you have Scott Weiland, Michael Jackson, Amy Winehouse, Prince, and Tom Petty. All dead, way too soon.

For these talented musicians, addiction was a losing cause that seemed insurmountable. In their despair, they retreated from the fight and took comfort in drugs or alcohol. And it keeps happening, even to this day.

Same goes for actors, artists, and so many other sensitive souls whose names were never known beyond their families and friends. Fighting addiction is never easy. A lot of times, it's a fight that can't be won—especially if you try to win it on your own.

But sometimes these stories have a different ending. Sometimes the battle can be won. Perhaps it takes more than one try—or a lot more than one try, when the odds are against you. But it canhappen.

People can realize that it's good to ask for help, that it takes a village to get sober. You can go to the meetings. Listen to others and their struggles. Allow yourself to be vulnerable. Say yes when someone offers to help.

You can learn humility. You can discover appreciation and gratitude. You can find faith and spirituality. People can work to get sober.

I know. I'm one of them.

It's funny looking back on that time in my life, those three years of complete insanity. On the one hand, I was at the top of my game. I was coming into my own as a snowboarder, headed for a potential career as a professional in a sport I loved. Think about that for a second: making bank for something you're passionate about, something you're good at—really good. That's every kid's dream come true. But then there was the other stuff, the stuff that kept taking me away from what I loved.

Sure, I was young and figuring things out, but it almost seems like it all happened to a different person. And in some ways, it did.

Some of my memories from that time are crystal clear, like they just happened the other day. Others are foggy, dulled by the passage of time or a handful of pharmaceuticals. It's hard enough to remember things when you're clear-headed. Can you imagine what it's like when you're high out of your mind?

No, go ahead—imagine it.

Really. I'll wait.

Too many recollections from those days are pretty much nonexistent for me. I was so messed up that I remember very little of what happened. That's where my mom comes in.

She lived through a lot of it too. My dad did what he could, but he was out of his league. Drugs and addiction were foreign territory for him—at least when it comes to dealing with it firsthand. But we'll get to him later.

It was really my mom who helped make a difference. She was the patient one, the outside observer, the steady hand—the one who had to step in sometimes and clean up the mess that my life had become. It wasn't easy, and some of her decisions might have been a little questionable to others. But she suffered through all of this for me, and she dedicated herself to being the best mom she could be.

When it comes right down to it, I might not even be here if it wasn't for her.

LAURA—

I will start with a confession of my own: I'm an addict too.

I am not a garden-variety alcoholic like you can find in most suburbs. I'm the kind who starts off with the early evening glass of Chardonnay, which inevitably leads to another glass or two—and that's just the warmup for dinner.

Since we're being truthful here, I had developed a taste for really nice wine, particularly those fabulous, full-bodied Cabernets that lined the shelves of our local specialty wine stores.

Call me a wine snob. I don't care. Maybe it's true, because I had to drink from a pretty glass, too—not a gaudy Marie Antoinette goblet or anything like that, but a proper stem glass with an air of elegance. I probably got that from my mother. It was always wine and always the good stuff. I never devolved to the point where I'd drink rotgut or anything unseemly.

Sure, I had a serious problem, but I still maintained standards. And rules.

No day-drinking. I didn't subscribe to the whole *It's five o'clock somewhere* notion. Nor did I hide bottles like some other alcoholics I know. While I often had an open bottle in the family room and another one in the kitchen, they were never kept secret. None of this pouring-minibar-bottles-into-a-coffee-cup-in-public nonsense. Thankfully, it never came to that.

Addiction comes in many forms. The damn disease is relentless and crosses every boundary known to man. It does not discriminate. I realize I'm not telling you anything new here. But alcohol, though just as destructive as other drugs, enjoys greater social acceptance in most circles. Sometimes it takes longer to address it for the ruinous force it really can be. To make matters worse, it's also so damn delicious.

While wine was definitely my go-to, I was no stranger to a good time when it came to drugs, either—at least in my youth. Still, alcohol can be found everywhere you turn, and it became my escape of choice.

It's probably in my genes. I could drink like a dock worker and cuss like one, too—something else I got from my mother. Mom was an absolute blast . . . until she wasn't.

Despite my reliance on alcohol, I've been told that I, too, was a lot of fun to be around. Once I was warmed up, I would become fearless. Stealing a Sno-Cat and grooming the slopes of

Vail, Colorado, is one of my more memorable events in my drunk-a-log. My behavior bordered on reckless but still managed to slip into the "fun" category. Until embarrassment reared its ugly, uninvited head yet again.

Like that time I celebrated a friend's fortieth birthday. Holy hell! We were at a restaurant that had a cozy country vibe—this was well before it was fashionable and before people used phrases like *farm-to-table*. That particular night, we drank more than our share. We weren't falling-down drunk, but we were drunk enough to climb onto the dinner table before the desserts arrived to compete in a chin-up contest using the closest rafter.

I was clearly in the lead, or at least I thought I was, but then I started to laugh. Laughter and chin-ups don't really go well together, so it was hard to maintain my grip on that exposed beam. The next thing I knew, I was falling back toward earth. Luckily, the dinner table was there to break my fall.

It broke too.

Miraculously, I wasn't hurt. The entire restaurant was startled into silence for a few moments before everyone burst out laughing. And laugh we did. I think my ribs hurt more from all the laughter than as a result of the fall. Keep in mind, I was a mom with four young boys at home, and I was the one acting like an adolescent.

In a strange way, this paralleled my son Tommy's behavior at age thirteen. Thankfully, he didn't have liquor in his life at that point. No, that would come a little later.

In some respects, Tommy and I grew up together. Our emotional maturity connected on some levels prior to my sobriety, and we share a similar sense of humor. We usually manage to find that silver lining even when things around us turn dark. But then again, as the Big Book—the book of Alcoholics Anonymous—says, "We are not a glum lot." Even in sobriety, we still have all kinds of crazy fun.

Like Tommy's, my addiction started at an early age. I had my historically wild moments in college and during my twenties. But in my case, it really didn't hit full stride until later in life. Like my son, I had to work to break through this powerful disease.

More on that later.

I was fortunate enough to be sober—thank God!—when Tommy began his own battle with addiction. That was a true gift: to be able to understand Tommy's situation, what he was going through. Had I been drinking, I would have been more frustrated and impatient with his drug and alcohol use. The Program helped me approach life on life's terms.

Sure, hindsight is 20/20, but my own experiences helped me get through this struggle and be there for my son. And that's what every mother wants, right? I'd paid my dues already, lived through my own fight, and come out the other side. I have done interventions and helped others, including my mother and a few other family members. But being the mother of the addict is a completely different challenge altogether.

As upsetting as Tommy's addiction was, I felt that I wanted to be there for him and help in the healthiest manner possible.

CHAPTER ONE

TOMMY—

Sometimes accepting help isn't as easy as it sounds. Sometimes you have to live with the pain, the never-ending cycle of disappointment. But then you realize: you're not alone. Not by a long shot. A lot of people helped me in my struggle with addiction. And that's one reason I wanted to put all this down on paper.

There's a lot of value in sharing your experiences. That's the whole idea behind group therapy: a collection of fuck-ups commiserating so you can sit there and not feel so bad about your own shit. If me sharing my story, my struggle, can help just one person, then it will be worth it. Those were definitely some dark days—in particular, one October night in 2012—when I wasn't sure how I was going to get out of it.

Let me tell you about that Halloween night.

It was a night like most others (for me, anyway)—drinking to excess, behaving like a newly escaped mental patient—except this one had everyone dressed up in their costumes. I think there was a full moon that night too, or maybe I just saw one in a Halloween poster somewhere. Or maybe I was so fucked up, I imagined the whole thing.

Drugs will do that.

Whatever it was, something was in the air. People were behaving like the moon cast some sort of crazy spell over them. I half expected hair to sprout from the backs of my hands and fangs to grow from my canines. And maybe they did. That might account for some of my monstrous behavior—and the torn, bloodied clothing I found the next morning.

There's something about Halloween that can bring out the worst in everyday people, so you can imagine what it does to an addict. Maybe it's the anonymity of dressing up and pretending to be someone you're not. Maybe it's the decorations that celebrate images of death and darkness. Or maybe it's the pumpkin spice lattes at Starbucks. Those are enough to make anyone want to destroy furniture.

I can almost see my lawyer pleading my case before a judge: *Your honor, my client can't be held responsible for his behavior. Have you seen the Halloween drinks from Starbucks?*

Or maybe the craziness is already there, and Halloween provides the perfect excuse to really go for it—to crank open the spigot of insanity and let everything come gushing out. The whole holiday is a license to act like a maniac under the pretense of acceptable, festive behavior, lightly flavored with pumpkin and spice.

This was exactly the kind of thinking that had me dressing up like Alex from *A Clockwork Orange*. For those unfamiliar with the movie, allow me to explain. The main character, Alex, is a homicidal menace to society—a young, sociopathic British hooligan, dressed all in white with a prominently displayed jockstrap worn on the *outside* of his clothes. Add to that black combat boots, a derby hat, a weapon-like cane, and a sinister leer, and you get the picture. That was me. That was Halloween.

The bizarre costume on its own would bolster the confidence of most guys my age. The temptation to behave like a complete jackass while mimicking the crazy character in the movie was irresistible to a twenty-one-year-old. When you factor in far too much alcohol and enough drugs to bring down a bull moose, you're asking for some serious trouble. And that's exactly what I got.

When I close my eyes, I can still see it.

Me, dressed like a homicidal maniac, running down Highway 40 through St. Louis, Missouri, into the blinding glow of oncoming headlights. Car horns bleating in the night. Angered motorists whipping past, hurling insults over the roar of their vehicles.

Me, sweating in the cool autumn night and, for some reason (okay, the drugs were the reason), not getting tired. Just the rhythmic slapping of my combat boots on the highway asphalt, before another car blows past in a violent gust of wind that lifts me from my feet. In the midst of the insanity, I lost my derby hat. Or maybe that was earlier, when I got punched out by a former Golden Gloves boxer. Losing the hat was the least of my worries.

It's a miracle I wasn't killed that night. Trust me, that shit's not for the faint of heart. At least not when you're sober, which I clearly wasn't.

But I wouldn't be doing the night justice if I didn't start at the beginning.

My buddy—let's call him Mark, because that was his name—picked me up that night, ready for the Halloween nonsense. Mark worked with me at the tennis club. Like me, he was an instructor and an all-round everyday guy who would do whatever boring shit the club needed done: mop the floor, take out the trash, string racquets, be nice to idiot customers when you felt like wringing their necks. You get it.

Mark shared my enthusiasm for a good time, but he didn't have quite the same propensity for overindulgence. Few do—not that I'm proud of it. At least not anymore.

Anyway, after ingesting a staggering mix of morphine, Xanax, and cocaine, we set off to some dive bar whose name I can't recall. You know the kind I'm talking about: the typical dark, roadhouse kind of place with faltering neon signs and reeking of spilled beer and stale cigarettes. Shitty top-forty songs from the nineties played on the sound system. Smokers—addicts in their own right, sucking nicotine into their lungs—clustered around the exit door, which was propped open with a wedge of folded cardboard from a beer case.

Mark and I, dressed like the degenerates from *A Clockwork Orange*, found a couple of vacant seats at the bar and pounded back a few quick drinks. It wasn't long before we started mixing it up with the locals, alcohol being the social lubricant that it is.

One of those locals stood out, even though there wasn't anything remarkable about him. He seemed like a typical blue-collar kid in his early twenties, the kind of guy who might've worked in his dad's repair shop. Except this guy couldn't keep his opinions to himself. Alcohol will do that.

He began to comment on the jockstrap worn outside of my white pants—or "trousers," as they say in the movie. I'm sure he must've felt he was being all clever, but his jokes weren't landing. The whole *Clockwork* reference was lost on this guy. I guess it's hard to find true movie buffs in a seedy place like that.

Anyway, this guy seemed fixated on my costume. Given that it was Halloween, you would normally cut some slack to a complete stranger dressed up like a movie character. But not this guy. He couldn't let go of it, and his relentless onslaught of bullshit was starting to kill my buzz.

Seriously. Knowing when to quit is a true talent, and this guy just didn't have it.

He kept at it. Mark tried his best to defuse the situation by going all Buddhist on him with kindness and compassion. He even offered to buy the douche a beer. But no. This guy wasn't having any of it. He was on the Asshole Express, and there was no stopping him.

This is precisely the moment when a reasonably sober person would've walked away. But *reasonable* and *sober* were two words that weren't in my vocabulary that night. I had to put a stop to this guy. I had to make him shut his mouth, so I did what any wasted, overconfident twenty-one-year-old would've done.

I took a swing.

Along with being a paid athlete, that's every young guy's fantasy: kicking ass in some bar that looks like a set from a Tarantino movie. Except in the fantasy, you connect with a meaty punch that knocks the a-hole from his barstool and sends him crashing to the floor. People cheer and buy you drinks. The girls swoon. Some awesome song comes on the jukebox, and you bask in the glory, being the warrior hero that you are.

That's the fantasy. That's the movie version.

The reality version is when you miss.

You wind up with all your might, like you're gonna separate this guy's head from his shoulders—except your haymaker whizzes by him and connects with nothing but air. The momentum from your own failed punch spins you off balance. And in that horrible second, that *Oh, fuck!* moment before it happens, you know you're in trouble. You're open. You're vulnerable. And you've already declared war.

Remember, you're also messed up—really messed up. That also has a tendency to slow things down.

So, while you might think that punch was destined to become

a finishing blow—the French have a term for this, and had I been paying attention in high school, I could have tossed that out and raised a few eyebrows—the reality was a little different. This guy could see my attempted punch coming from a good mile away, in plenty of time to lean back out of the way.

Then time really did slow. He looked at me like he knew something I didn't, which was probably true. And the fucker cold-cocked me—a clean, undefended punch right to my face. And it really fucking hurt.

Nothing like some good, old ultra-violence to startle you from your buzz.

The next thing I knew, the bar started to tip sideways. The whole place inverted with a crash, and suddenly I was on that filthy floor, and it really did smell like week-old beer. The cracked tiles seemed unnaturally clear, and as if the smell weren't bad enough, they were sticky against my cheek.

I could hear Mark and some other people yelling. A couple of the barflies apparently found this whole thing hilarious. Their uproarious laughter filled my ears, right over the ringing from the punch. I groped at my mouth and pulled my hand back to see it glistening with my own blood.

Finally, I found my way to my hands and knees. Someone grabbed hold of my shirt and hoisted me to my feet. The blood on my hand looked surreal against the white of my outfit, like maybe this really *was* a movie. I was still unsteady, and the room hadn't stopped moving.

Spinning rooms. Hate those.

Mark must've ushered me out to his car, as my next memory is of resting my head against the open window of his rusted Corolla while he drove away. The cool wind felt good and allowed me to forget momentarily that my face was pretty banged up. It had been a hell of a punch, and the floor must've hit me pretty hard too.

If I hadn't been so wasted, I would've recognized that the night was off to a bad start. But the pain hadn't managed to break through the comfort barrier provided by the drugs.

After we drove on for a few minutes, I convinced Mark to let me out of the car. Not exactly known for his good judgment, he agreed, and I set off into the night on foot, still dressed like a British hooligan, covered in blood. I was on my way to see my ex-girlfriend, who'd just broken up with me. It seemed like a good time to show up at her door and convince her to take me back. I mean, why not?

On my way to her apartment, I passed under a bridge, where I came across a homeless guy pushing a shopping cart that brimmed with his worldly possessions. He looked younger than I imagined a homeless guy should look, and that seemed to be a good enough reason for me to stop and speak with him.

Another bad decision in a night full of them.

The conversation remains vague, and I'll blame the drugs. The talk soon turned ugly, and I'll blame myself. The guy even warned me to leave him alone, but I didn't listen. He professed to be a former Golden Gloves boxer, but I still didn't listen. I countered his threat and warned him that I was a tennis instructor at the tennis club. He didn't seem particularly impressed.

Neither of us would back down. Soon, although I'm not exactly sure how we got there, we arrived at the point of no return. I guess he'd had enough of me running off at the mouth and decided to do what he did best.

It was a punch I never saw coming.

And guess what? The guy really was a Golden Gloves boxer.

Those fuckers know how to hit. It's different from a regular punch by some regular ass-wipe in a dive bar. Boxers know how to put their weight into it. The force is many times greater than the force of a normal punch. And this one was delivered with precision.

A shot to the solar plexus doubled me over, knocking the wind out of me. I clutched my gut and tried to suck some air back into my lungs. But before I could even draw a breath, he let loose a second shot: an uppercut to the face. It took me right off my feet. I saw more stars than the Hubble Space Telescope, then crashed against the sidewalk.

For the second time in as many hours, I was on the ground, bleeding. Moaning, curled up in the fetal position, I tried to say something defiant. Fortunately, the homeless guy had had enough. He returned to his squeaky shopping cart and ambled off into the night. I think he was even whistling "Singin' in the Rain" from *A Clockwork Orange.*

Kubrick fans. You never know where you're gonna find them.

Once I was able to collect myself, I returned to my original mission: to find my ex and win her back. Me and bad decisions—we just couldn't get enough of each other.

After the marathon run down Highway 40, I arrived at Sarah's apartment. It was one of those cheap, neglected, two-story brick places that students clamor to rent because it's all they can afford. Yet even a shithole like this had some sort of security measures: in this case, a laughably low fence that would hardly deter an eighty-five-year-old paraplegic.

When Sarah wouldn't buzz me through, I hopped the flimsy gate and trudged right up to her door. After a lot of pleading and fist-banging, I noticed a fire extinguisher on the nearby wall. It was encased in glass that wasn't supposed to be broken except in the event of an emergency. And obviously, Sarah's refusal to let me in constituted an emergency, at least in my books.

I decided to punch that glass case with all I had. Maybe it was the punch I wished I'd thrown earlier—at either one of my adversaries—but this one was directed at a perfectly innocent fire extinguisher. Somehow I felt the need to liberate the poor thing. The glass shattered and tinkled to the pavement.

I stood there, breathing heavily and examining the gaping cuts in my knuckles. The blood began to pulse from my open wounds, and suddenly this didn't seem like the wisest of decisions.

Sarah must have heard the sound of breaking glass, because she finally opened the door. She stood there looking at me with a debilitating mix of pity and contempt, but no real horror. She probably thought all the blood was that syrupy stuff that comes out of a plastic squeeze bottle—a part of my Halloween costume.

I tried to launch into the speech I'd rehearsed on the way over, but it didn't come out the way I wanted. My thoughts weren't clear, and I wasn't making much sense.

She countered my argument with a litany of incidents where I'd fucked up. And the list was long—really long. I suspect I would've had enough time to trot off to Starbucks for a pumpkin latte, but instead I stood there and took it like a man. I let her say her piece. What else was I gonna do?

I do remember the look on her face, and that really said it all. It was over. She'd had enough, and she deserved better. It was tough to disagree. She was calm about it, though—the adult on the apartment steps. And when she gently closed the door on me, I felt even worse than before.

What was I expecting—that suddenly all of my bad behavior would be forgiven? That she'd take me back with open arms and try to work through this mess with me? Sure, maybe if we were living in a movie. But not here. Not in this reality that had become my life.

As I retreated from Sarah's apartment, I discovered my phone had managed to remain in my possession. Once I got over the shock, I dialed Mark. Ten minutes later, I was back in his car.

We drove over to his place, looking to cap the night with a few more drinks. I started making some calls in search of a final party or two. Before this got too far, though, Mark decided it wasn't the best idea and suggested that we call it a night.

"You've had enough," he said. "You're a mess." I don't think he was too fond of the blood I'd smeared on his sofa, either. Spray 'n Wash will only do so much.

Mark kindly offered to drive me home, but like most addicts worth their salt, I wasn't ready to throw in the towel. Daylight was still a good two or three hours away. Surely there was more fun to be had, somewhere. All we had to do was look for it.

"Dude, come on," he implored. "You need to get some sleep."

Those are the last words any addict wants to hear.

We argued. Mark, to his credit, held firm. Things escalated. Frustration had been on a slow simmer for the entire night, and now it just exploded to the surface. He said some shit he probably shouldn't have said, and finally I snapped. I totally lost control.

I grabbed Mark by his arms and lifted him off his feet, like some crazed defensive tackle. I had a pretty good head of steam and carried him across the room while he yelled in protest.

We charged through the open sliding doors, out to the narrow terrace. I slammed Mark up against the balcony rail. He flailed in desperation, his fingers clawing at my face, but it wasn't enough. My rage was pure. I was blinded by it—and fueled by the drugs.

In the next instant, I heaved him over the rail.

Chapter One

For an eternal half second, Mark looked at me in total disbelief. Then he hit the pavement below with a sickening crunch.

Gasping for air, I stared down at his unmoving body. My knuckles were white on the rail as I leaned over, shocked by my own behavior.

Mark still wasn't moving.

I started to freak out. This wasn't how the movie was supposed to go. What was I going to do? Become a fugitive? Dressed like this?

Nobody was supposed to die.

What the fuck had I done?

How had things gotten so out of control?

CHAPTER TWO

LAURA—

Maybe it runs in the family, but Halloween hasn't been kind to either Tommy or me. I guess it's hard to blame a whacked-out holiday for the havoc it wreaks on one's life, but some seriously bad behavior can happen on that night in particular. Coincidentally or not, Halloween was my last drunk hurrah too.

But before we get to that defining moment in my own battle with addiction, let me provide a little context.

I always get a little pissed off when I see someone doing something really stupid, like texting and driving. In the grand scheme of things, it's not as egregious as, say, drinking too much tequila and running the *Exxon Valdez* aground. But still . . . it's up there.

What's with the texting and driving? What's so important that you need to fumble with your phone while at the wheel of a 5,000-pound vehicle, traveling 100 feet per second? Can't it wait? Who's so important that they require an immediate response? If you aren't watching the road and staying focused while you are driving, you're just begging for something bad to happen. Common sense and courtesy would dictate a different course of action. If it really is important, the least you can do is pull over and text from the safety of the roadside.

All of this sounds completely rational to a responsible person. However, if you've been steadily drinking for hours on end, and you have consumed enough wine to fill—oh, I don't know, maybe an Eric Javits hat box, then common sense and rationality tend to take a back seat. It's amazing, the effect alcohol has on one's reasoning. It's like reasoning itself has this fragile veil that's easily washed away with a few good swallows of Cabernet Sauvignon.

But let's get back to Halloween. This would've been 2008. And I'm not going to tell you I remember it like it was yesterday, because that's simply not true. I do remember a lot of it, though—certainly enough to share here.

The night started off harmlessly enough, as most Halloweens do. All intentions were in the right place: the kids, the costumes, the house decorations, the carved pumpkins, the huge bowls of candy for trick-or-treaters. I had donned my shiny black witch's outfit and, after a visit with my mother at her assisted living facility, I later joined Tom (my husband) and Billy (my youngest) at our friend Meredith's house.

Halloween at Meredith's had become a tradition, eight years running. Even though Meredith was newly sober, she was still tremendous fun to be around. The party was what'd I'd expect from her—fabulous, in a way that most of her parties tend to be: good wine, horrible food, fun friends, great chat.

Most of us were in costume that night—nothing too outlandish, but plenty of fun to be had. One friend, Tony, was dressed as a nun with a five o'clock shadow. Another friend wore lederhosen. The kids kept themselves busy while the elders enjoyed a little time to socialize. Eventually the dads would take the chilluns trick-or-treating, allowing the moms a "hall pass" to get hammered. And get hammered we did. Or maybe I was the only one hammered and didn't realize it.

It was a party like so many others, until this one took a surprise turn into the midst of a very frank conversation on alcoholism.

Keep in mind, this wasn't a common topic at our dinner parties, where we drank socially for, well, social reasons. But for some reason it emerged that night in my conversation with Meredith. Perhaps it was her newfound sobriety, or perhaps my inhibitions had been softened by wine, but we soon found ourselves discussing the topic at length.

Curious, I asked Meredith, "How did you know it was time to quit drinking?" What I really meant was: *How does one know when one is an alcoholic?*

Meredith took a long moment before answering, staring into the bubbles of her Perrier. "You just know," she said finally.

Hmm. Not exactly the answer I was looking for.

Later I would realize her response was true to the Program principle of *attraction, not promotion.* But right then, even though I was a little drunk, I think I knew deep down that I had a problem. By asking Meredith how she knew it was time to take action, I was looking for an answer—for confirmation that perhaps I, too, had a problem. It was becoming more obvious that I, like my dear friend, was an alcoholic. With that question—*How does one know?*—I was seeking the answer I was secretly hoping to hear.

It was an answer I wouldn't find just yet.

That Halloween night was one of the first times I openly acknowledged that I had a problem. I even went as far as suggesting to someone at the party that I needed to get sober—a strange admission from an alcoholic yet to do the work, especially while I was buzzed.

I must've raised some concern from my friends, but they were too polite to mention it. Most of them dismissed the notion in their good-natured way, even when it came to something like taking away my car keys. That's the last thing any of them would attempt, although some had been known to follow me home. Like that would somehow keep me safe.

Wrestling car keys from an intoxicated person is tough enough. Try it with a full-blown alcoholic. That requires a whole other level of courage, the kind usually reserved for those Florida park attendants with fake Aussie accents who hop into a pit with an eleven-foot alligator.

Add the social constraints of our lovely circle of friends, with all the concern for appearance and decorum, and you have a clear path to disaster. No one ever made that move. No one was willing to say, "Laura, let me call you a taxi."

Not that I'm blaming anyone else—certainly not. The mistakes were mine and mine alone.

And I chalked up another mistake late that Halloween night when, armed with a determination to return home to hit the hay, I staggered out into the brisk fall night.

Somehow my car keys found their way into the ignition of my vehicle—no easy task when you're inebriated. The car started exactly like it's supposed to, and I headed home, a bleary-eyed witch speeding through the night in command of her SUV broom. It's not a long drive, and I had made it several million times. I could have driven it with my eyes closed—and that was part of the problem.

So, I'm humming along with the heat turned up (hey, even witches get cold), and then I hear the chime. It's the iPhone chime, the one that announces you have a text—the one that evokes a Pavlovian response that says, *Stop what you're doing. Your immediate attention is required. Never mind whatever activity you're in the midst of.*

It's a good thing I was a witch that night and not the captain of an oil tanker.

Now, you may be familiar with an internal monologue that goes something like this:

It's a text! For me!

Who could it be? Who's texting me at this hour?

Is it important? An emergency?

Not an emergency, you hope. Only one way to find out. You fish the phone out of your cupholder and raise it to your eyes. You squint through that dull fog of Cabernet and begin to read. Then you tap out your response with your thumb, fumbling, while your other hand remains planted on the steering wheel. And don't forget, you're traveling 100 feet per second inside a 5,000-pound metallic projectile.

If disaster does have a recipe, I had put together a pretty impressive list of ingredients. I still shudder at the thought of it.

Hopefully, your experience with texting while driving turned out better than mine. Hopefully, you hadn't been drinking. But in my case, what happened next is anyone's guess. All I know is this: I awoke inside the car, still strapped into my seatbelt, to something pressing up against my face. It took a minute for me to realize the airbags had deployed.

I remember fragments of those next few moments, but they're seriously distorted by my indulgence from that night. A few memories didn't come back until well into the next day, when I began to piece things together.

Shaking my head like a dog with water in its ears, I released my belt restraint and tried to shove the airbag away. No easy task. I still had traces of powder from the airbag on my face, and my head hurt like hell.

A disembodied voice broke through my haze of confusion.

"Mr. Boldt, are you all right?"

Was this some kind of hallucination? A joke?

"Mr. Boldt?" asked the voice again.

They say God has a sense of humor. Was He screwing with me? If not, why was He looking for my husband?

Then it dawned on me. It wasn't the voice of God. It was the voice of OnStar, the vehicle's communication and safety system.

"Mr. Boldt?"

"He's not here right now," I said. I almost added, *Can I take a message?*

Disoriented, I didn't know where I was, how I got there, or what was going on—not the best combination of bewilderment. What I did know was, I was no longer moving. The Escalade had come to an abrupt, unintentional stop that likely had something to do with some very nasty but basic physics.

"We saw that you had an accident," the voice said.

"You did?"

That was amazing. For a second, I wondered what else they could see. The all-seeing OnStar seemed a little more divine than I would have imagined.

"Would you like us to send an ambulance?" came the voice.

"No, thanks. I'm fine. Really."

The last thing I needed was an ambulance. That would likely entail a police report, and I wasn't about to blow into a breathalyzer.

It took a little convincing, but the OnStar angel decided to grant my wish and click off in search of the next imperiled driver. With that taken care of, I returned to the task at hand.

While fussing to push the airbags out of my face, I was able to restart the behemoth SUV and make my way back to the road. It wasn't easy.

Don't get me wrong. Airbags are a wonderful invention, and one probably had just saved my life. I just prefer when it's still packed tightly into its hidden compartment as opposed to deployed and chafing my chin as I reach around it to grip the steering wheel.

I suppose a sober person wouldn't dream of this kind of absurd behavior, of driving home after an accident, fingertips barely reaching the wheel. The whole thing felt embarrassing, ridiculous—kind of like trying to hug an adult walrus.

Then comes the part of the night that falls into the blackout category. For the life of me, I have no idea what happened. It's as though someone managed to erase that slice of time from my memory. Somehow I found my way home to the comfort of my bed, and I awoke a little while later to my phone buzzing on the nightstand.

My bedside clock told me it was 4 a.m.

Who the hell is calling at this hour? I wondered, grabbing the phone to answer it.

My son Peter.

That pang to the heart.

Oh, dear . . . It's every mother's worst fear: the dreaded 4 a.m. call.

"Peter, are you okay?" I asked

"Yes. I just don't feel very well."

I slumped in relief. *Yes* is my favorite response to *Are you okay?*

"I want to come home," Peter continued. His fourteen-year-old voice sounded so little, so vulnerable.

"Okay, honey. I'm on my way." Summoning my inner reserves of mom-strength, I willed myself out of bed and downstairs. What I found shocked me: the SUV had been haphazardly abandoned in the driveway, half demolished.

"What the—"

I was furious. *Which one of my boys did this?* I thought. *Who took the car without my permission?* I was tempted to wake Tommy from his sleep and demand answers, but that would have to wait. For now, I had to get Peter.

I'd like to think I wasn't drunk at that point, but it's difficult to say.

I returned to the house in search of the keys for the other car. Unable to find them, I had no choice but to wake my husband. After studying the wreck that used to be our SUV, Tom looked at me, incredulous.

"What happened?" he asked, as concerned as I was.

This seemed to be the running question, and I didn't really have an answer. All I knew was that Peter wasn't feeling well and he needed his mother. Few duties are more sacred. Solving the Mystery of the Destroyed SUV would have to wait. I took the keys to Tom's green Jeep, and off I went.

That morning was like a million other mornings in the life of an alcoholic. You drift back to reality through the hazy aftermath of your binge drinking. Your throat is dry, coated with the sour aftertaste of alcohol, and your strength is nowhere to be found. We've all been there, but most without the frequency that had become far too familiar for me.

I know a lot of alcoholics who have tried-and-true remedies after a night of drinking. Some concoct weird, sludgy potions of seaweed protein and other ridiculous ingredients that can be found only in the deepest, darkest recesses of Whole Foods.

Me? My remedy for a night of overindulgence was simple: I liked to exercise. I held fast to the belief that if I could simply sweat it out, my stamina would miraculously regenerate and I'd be ready to go again later.

Drink, run, repeat. Simple.

Part of me thought that if I ran, I wasn't really an alcoholic. After all, how many alcoholics could clock the miles I did and feel like a million bucks afterward? Not many, I'm willing to guess. I was in that rarefied group of alcoholics who didn't often succumb to hangovers as mere mortals did—much to the chagrin of other drinkers. My biggest obstacle was the inevitable brain fog that I couldn't quite outrun the morning after.

As they say in the Program, it's your new normal.

I also found myself incredibly slow to perform basic motor functions. This started to become a concern because, as everyone knows, being a mom has its own list of demands. Despite my post-drinking slowness, I still had to make breakfast for the kids, drive them to school, and put out any fires that might arise with a brood of four growing boys. These responsibilities couldn't be neglected, no matter what. And I believe it was the weight of this responsibility that propelled me to take the next important step.

Staring at the wreck of my car, I realized that it had been me driving the SUV on Halloween night, and that it was a miracle I hadn't killed someone, including myself. That was when I asked myself: *What am I doing?*

If there was a defining moment in my journey to sobriety, it began with an epiphany that morning: I needed to get sober.

A distinct feeling overcame me, gut-wrenching and more powerful than anything I'd ever felt. On all levels, it was spiritual—a clear sign that God was doing for me what I couldn't do for myself.

How many times had He tried to reach me? This time was different. This time I heard Him.

And I knew I had to change. If not now, then when? The feeling was so powerful that it filled me with relief. The fear evaporated. I embraced this horrific event for what it was: a truly divine gift.

I went back inside to face Tom. We sat down, and I told him plainly, "I'm an alcoholic. I need to stop drinking."

He looked at me for a long moment without responding. Finally, he said, "I'm not ready."

"Ready? Ready for what?"

"I have to admit, I am concerned. But I'm not ready to tell you to stop." Tom didn't have firsthand experience with addiction, but he had grown up with a physician father who did. His father, also named Tom, founded Edgewood, a sobriety center, because he had a close friend who couldn't stay sober. It was this kind of compassion that helped shape Tom into the man who stood before me, asking, "Do you think you can control your drinking?"

He wasn't ready for my assessment, to accept that I was indeed an alcoholic with a serious problem. It wasn't until much later that he admitted his relief in that moment.

Tom has always been a glass-half-full kind of guy—he always finds the positive and sees the good in people. And I love him for it. But he was blindsided by my startling declaration. That day, he gave credence to the old joke: denial is not just a river in Egypt.

Undeterred, I knew it was now or never.

Less than two days later—November 3, 2008—I began the Program. I came to embrace it slowly but surely. AA became an integral part of my universe and changed my life. And today, I often think of that great C. S. Lewis quote: *You can't go back and change the beginning, but you can start where you are now and change the ending.*

CHAPTER THREE

TOMMY—

My mom has that superhero virtue. I'm not talking about deflecting bullets with bracelets or any of that shit, but the kind that allows you to quit cold turkey and stay the course. That was something she didn't hand down to me. My path was different. My Halloween hangover was different, too.

I awoke like that guy in *The Godfather*. You know the one I'm talking about—the old dude in satin pajamas with the gray fifties hairdo that still looks good even though he's just been asleep. He's groggy, and when he pushes back the sheets of his ginormous bed, he discovers he's covered in blood. Yeah, blood. Blood from a horse's head.

And me? My hair's pointing in every direction known to man, and I'm still in costume from last night. No satin pajamas for this guy. But I am covered in blood, except that it's not from a horse's head. It's from a horse's ass.

Me.

Like a lot of addicts who crash from their high, I was left with a horrible sinking feeling that morning. If the alcohol and drugs don't make you want to puke, that horrible feeling will—that crippling sense of dread when you have to ask yourself, *What did I do?*

Chapter Three

Once that question was out there, the pieces from the previous night began tumbling down into my consciousness like unwanted, steaming shards of truth. They were the first flurries of the coming shitstorm.

What exactly happened last night? Was anybody hurt? How did I get home? Where's my wallet? What happened to the rest of my teeth? Why am I here and not in county jail? Did the Cardinals come back in the ninth?

Those were just a few of the questions swimming around in my pounding head. But first, coffee. I needed something, anything, to help clear my head and get me back on my feet—or at least on the sofa, where I could shield my eyes from the morning sun, listen to SportsCenter, and try to figure things out.

After a fifteen-minute search, I found my phone and checked my messages. They weren't good. A text from Sarah—short, sweet, and genuinely concerned—asked if I made it home okay. The text was just pithy enough, without encouraging me to believe there might be hope. She struck that perfect balance of reminding me what a great person she is and how badly I screwed up in destroying our relationship.

Sarah still cared about me, and she couldn't change that. I messed up, and she couldn't change that either. I texted back to let her know I was still alive and left it at that. If nothing else, I had to respect her wishes.

Nothing from Mark, though, and I was starting to remember why.

The coffee helped remove some of the cobwebs. Still, that relentless jackhammer beat pounded away at my memory, not to mention my temples. Think of it as the Barry Bonds of hangovers, steroids included. Even my eyes hurt from the light.

Man, that was a rough one, I thought, still trying to find some clarity.

Maybe I had been turned into a vampire and didn't yet know it. Or maybe I just needed some hair of the dog that had raised its leg and fouled my Halloween night. Both were distinct possibilities. Not much I could do about the former, but the latter . . .

I found just what I needed in the bottom pocket of my backpack: a couple of leftover pills that somehow had managed to escape being ingested. After rubbing off the backpack lint and some other unidentified stuff, I slugged the pills back with the coffee (now cold) and waited for them to take hold.

Relief was on the way, thanks to the hardworking chemists at some of America's finest pharmaceutical companies. The hair of the dog—yes, sir.

I wanted to call Mark but was afraid of what I might learn. Was he even alive?

The fact that I wasn't in police custody was probably a good sign, but I couldn't count on that alone. It was still early. The cops around that neighborhood weren't known for their lightning-quick response times. Dogtown is a funky section of St. Louis—formerly a community of Irish coal miners in the 1800s, but now an affordable place for young people to live, stocked with corner bars and bakeries. While homicides weren't all that common, I didn't want to be the guy to change all that.

The idea of waiting around to learn my fate wasn't all that appealing. I had to take matters into my own hands. I had to find out more. After surrendering control to a night of drug-induced insanity, it felt good to take the reins of destiny and steer them in a different direction. At least for a little while.

I drove my motorcycle to Mark's place, and when I got there, the blinds were drawn and all was quiet. I gathered my courage and knocked. Nothing. I tried again. Still nothing. I even shouted through the closed window for him to open the door. One of the neighbors peered out from behind her curtains, scowling at me like I was a toilet brush salesman.

If Mark was inside, he didn't want me to know.

Unsure of what to do next, I decided to revisit the last place I'd seen him—the scene of the crime, so to speak.

The pavement below Mark's balcony.

I'm not sure what I was expecting. I only hoped it wouldn't be the chalk outline of Mark's body on the pavement, like some murder scene from a cheesy TV show.

Nope, no chalked body drawing. No police tape or photographers. So far, so good.

Even the neighbors remained in their apartments, carrying on with their lives. It was as though nobody gave a shit but me. I was okay with that. But as I stepped closer, my worst fears seemed to be confirmed. I had come to that part of the movie when the soundtrack is interrupted by an over-the-top orchestral sting.

There was blood.

At least, I assumed it was blood—or maybe some other rust-colored, coagulated stuff that had mostly seeped into the cracks of the uneven parking lot surface. I tried to rub it away with the sole of my sneaker, as if that would somehow change what had happened last night. Another exercise in futility. It had become my specialty.

The more I looked at the stain, the more it looked like blood.

Shit. This wasn't good.

What had happened to my friend?

Did he cheat the throes of death, scrape himself off the pavement, and limp to the nearest hospital? Probably not.

Had he risen from the dead and started wandering Dogtown, looking to feast on human brains? Not likely.

Was his carcass dragged off by a pack of ravenous wild animals? Unlikely, given that this was still the city of St. Louis, after all. I suppose the wild animals could have escaped from the zoo, but I'd still have to put that one in the long-shot column.

After a good twenty minutes of drug-hampered speculation, I was no closer to the truth. I needed to do something, and I needed to do it now.

But what?

The answer was right in front of me the whole time, nestled deep in the pocket of my jeans. Worried that my quest might take longer than planned, I'd had the good foresight to bring along some precautionary measures: good old morphine, the breakfast of champions.

That helped take the edge off my worry and allowed me to focus. Having seen enough detective shows, I knew with reasonable certainty what my next move had to be. Armed with this sudden sense of purpose, I went to the hospital to see if I could find my friend.

Leaning against the information desk counter, acting all *CSI* and shit, I put on my best game face and inquired as to whether Mark had checked in. I was smooth, I was poised, I was good. *Suave* is probably too strong a word, but you get the picture.

A rather bored-looking receptionist asked me to spell Mark's full name and then scoured a patient list.

It took forever, or maybe only a few seconds. In that time, I went from being a prime-time detective guy to being a sweaty outlaw. Thankfully, the drugs helped ease my worries and keep my fears in check.

Finally, the receptionist looked up from her list. Mark had not been admitted—not here, at least. I almost asked her to check the morgue but thought better of it. Why tempt fate? Nothing harshes your buzz like a friend's dead body.

I was about to leave when a nearby nurse gazed up from some charts, her face creased in concern. She assessed me a moment with her professional eye before asking, "Sir, are you all right?"

I did the whole *Who, me?* routine, then turned and ran like I'd forgotten a cake in the oven. I'm not sure why, but that seemed to be the right choice at the time.

Back outside, my pulse returned to normal—well, normal for me, given the stuff coursing through my veins. I made my way to the tennis club, hoping Mark wasn't seriously hurt and had reported for work. Wishful thinking, right?

Completely breaking club rules, I parked in the preferred guest spaces—taking up two, in fact. Not easy to pull off when parking a motorcycle. Add that to my list of talents.

In the lobby of the tennis club, I almost tripped over the wet vac extension cord before stumbling upon Zach, who sat on his perch behind the front desk, texting while he alternated between breathing with his mouth open and chewing a burrito. Mouth breathers always throw me for a loop, and this guy was no exception. Not very forgiving of me, I guess. Who knows? Maybe he had a cold.

"Zach!" I cried.

He slowly raised his eyes from his iPhone, looking put out by my sudden intrusion.

"You seen Mark?" I asked.

Zach looked incredulous for a full ten-count, then replied through a mouthful of food, "Dude. You haven't heard?"

My heart sank. "Heard what?"

"He's totally f'd up." Zach hated to swear. Maybe it was a Christian thing. "Called in sick. Or at least his sister did. That's where he's staying—her place."

I could breathe again. At least I wasn't a murderer.

"Guy can't really talk. He's heavily medicated," Zach continued. "Mark took a swan dive off his balcony—at least, that's what she thinks."

I was speechless too, but grateful Mark was still alive. Zach went back to his burrito and mouth breathing. I had more important things to worry about. It dawned on me that I had a problem—a serious problem.

I decided I really needed to do something.

LAURA—

The circumstances surrounding these episodes of near disaster only made things that much more difficult—not only for Tommy, but for the whole family.

My mother, Mary Margaret, was ill with Parkinson's and dementia. That's a powerful one-two. We had recently moved her to an assisted-living facility, Sunrise—a name that conveys hope, friendliness, and new beginnings. She loved the place, and they were so wonderful with her. It got to the point where she needed around-the-clock care, so this was the place for her to be.

It was heartbreaking to watch Mom slowly deteriorate the way she did. Sometimes I didn't even recognize her. She had become so detached most of the time, she didn't recognize me as her daughter. At times she even thought I was her mother. Dementia is such an awful state, so completely cruel and unfair.

But I would never get frustrated with her. Some people did, and it was so hurtful. There was something childlike about the way she behaved, especially as the dementia worsened. At night, she'd wander around, sometimes leaving the facility altogether. Her newfound innocence and curiosity seemed insatiable.

Yet somehow, through most of this, she managed to maintain her poise and elegance. She'd still find the time to put on her makeup and Hermès scarves. It seemed like a small act of defiance against the breakdown of her mind and body.

We did the best we could for Mom. Sunrise allowed us to bring in some of her furniture, to make the surroundings more comfortable and maybe even a little familiar. My visits with her were sweet, full of laughter, and often playful, as though I was suddenly the adult and she was the child. Sometimes Mom just needed to feel safe, and I would respond by being with her until her fears passed.

Her needs had become simple. During the day, she was perfectly happy to lounge around in her bathrobe and sip Diet Coke to wash back her toast. Mom was also in the Program for many years, and somehow she was able to remember that she didn't drink. Her caregiver even took her to meetings. They were that important to her.

It wasn't only Mom's illness weighing down on our family. My stepfather, Al, had just suffered a heart attack. Al was no longer married to my mother, but he and I were still incredibly close. He was so good to me while I was growing up that our bond never weakened.

After his heart attack, we decided to have Al move in with us. Talk about a challenge. Al could be very demanding when it came right down to it, but he was always so appreciative. Strangely, this time became a highlight in our relationship. I wound up camping out in his room sometimes, and we talked well into the night, like little kids happily conspiring during a sleepover.

Tommy and his brothers were fascinated by having Al live with us. They helped take care of him, and I think it taught them some valuable lessons that only strengthened our family.

Thank goodness for that! We were going to need it.

Still, my mother's decline on its own would have been upsetting enough. Add the rest of the family circus, and you have the perfect cocktail for complete disaster. People can relapse over far less than this, but I stayed close to my program of recovery, and I felt armed for whatever came my way.

TOMMY—

What I needed to do was find Mark and apologize. That was my only thought now. I returned to my motorcycle, pleased to see it was right where I'd left it outside the tennis club. Not a tow truck in sight.

After a few phone calls, I tracked down his sister. Her place was twenty minutes away from the club—or six minutes on a motorcycle, but I didn't see the point in attracting the attention of the police. Sure, I was in control—maintaining, as it were—but why tempt fate? I'd had enough of that for several lifetimes.

I had somehow managed to stay out of jail this long. No point in courting disaster.

Arriving at Mark's sister's place, I parked my bike and sauntered up to the door. I lifted my fist to knock but hesitated, suddenly feeling like I should've brought some kind of peace offering. Mark wasn't exactly the get-well-soon-flowers type, so maybe . . . chocolates? Or better yet, PlayStation had a new—

The door swung open before I could finish my thought.

I stood there, busted. An addict in the headlights. "Hey, Melissa," I said, smiling nervously.

"Marissa," she corrected me.

"Really? I always thought your name—"

"What do you want, Tommy?" She didn't seem happy to see me at all. Hardly any way to treat her brother's best friend.

"I'm here to see Mark," I declared. "I was going to bring flowers, but I know Mark's not—"

She closed the door in my face before I could finish my bullshit rap. Perceptive, that woman.

This whole door-being-closed-in-my-face thing was fast becoming a pattern. "C'mon, Marissa. Let me see Mark."

"He's sleeping."

Then the door opened again. She could barely hide her contempt. If looks could kill, I'd be on the ground.

"I know what you did," Marissa said in an angry whisper.

"You do?"

She continued to glare at me, her eyes piercing me with daggers.

"Which part, exactly?" I asked, nervous to hear which damning example of my shitty behavior she was preparing to fling back at me.

"You know what I'm talking about." Her face quivered as she struggled to control her anger.

"Actually, I did so many awful things last night, you're gonna have to help me."

Calming herself, she exhaled in resignation. Then she closed the door a second time.

His sister was silent. At least one of us knew when to quit.

To my relief, he was not dead but very much alive. I found out later he had a concussion, mild scrapes, and some bruises. I had dodged a huge bullet. I was scared shitless for him and for me.

Back at home, my mom seemed surprised to see me in such awful shape. Before she could even ask, I volunteered, "Rough night."

She nodded in agreement, waiting for more. Her eyes were filled with that look of mom-worry.

"I think I broke my hand," I said, raising my swollen mitt.

"What happened to your teeth?" she asked, stepping closer. There was a calm to her that was mildly reassuring, but I could still detect deep concern over my self-destructive behavior.

"I got into a fight. Maybe two."

She remained quiet, as though unsure of how to respond. But the expression on her face—that *Oh, Tommy, what have you done?* look—was like another punch I couldn't deflect.

"I need some help," I finally admitted.

She didn't disagree.

"Will you help me?"

She hugged me in response. A good mom-hug where the world suddenly seemed like a slightly better place.

"Of course I will," she said.

"I'll do whatever it takes," I said. And I meant it.

LAURA—

Tommy's willingness to go to rehab was a huge relief. Until that moment, part of me still wasn't fully aware of how bad it was with Tommy. Thankfully, I entered the situation already sober. Things were challenging enough without Tommy being in the clutches of addiction.

Getting back to the hot spot in time while Tommy was actively using, our lives seemed as though a hellacious tornado had hit our family.

Sadly, Mom died soon after Al came to stay with us.

But the craziness didn't stop there.

Al's current wife, Charlotte, suddenly became unglued. She had married Al when I was only twelve and had welcomed me into her life. I adored her, and we became good friends through the years.

Over time, I came to realize that Charlotte struggled with her own inner demons. She seemed to suffer from personality disorders and OCD. That likely explained some of her wild mood swings, from elation to the deepest depths of depression. The helplessness was her greatest obstacle. She was in so much emotional pain—a kind of pain that most of us are unable to fathom. It was so sad for all of us, and most significantly for Charlotte.

Once Al's health began to decline, Charlotte became bitter. She refused to have Al live with her, because she didn't want to have his nurses in the house. But she also was a little jealous that we didn't consult her about his day-to-day care. She would routinely collapse on the floor and complain that no one was paying attention to her.

Soon, she was on an unstable, downward spiral into darkness.

Although Charlotte had been diagnosed with breast cancer, the prognosis was good. Her chances of survival were excellent after she elected to have a mastectomy. But what should have been good news wasn't enough to stop what happened next.

I'm still not exactly sure what specifically was going through Charlotte's mind that day, and I guess none of us will ever know. She was so anxious, so lost and riddled with helplessness. Ultimately she decided the pain was too much to bear, and she took her own life with a single bullet. It was every bit as horrible as it sounds.

It was an emotionally crazy time, and our whole family was dealing with a smorgasbord of feelings: anger, sadness, compassion, and even relief. I truly cared for Charlotte, even as her world crumbled before our eyes—before Tommy's eyes. Tommy adored her, and the feeling was mutual. Eventually I came to the point of forgiving Charlotte for taking her own life—and for the demanding and dark circumstances surrounding her suicide.

First Mom, then Charlotte. The shock and sorrow were almost too much. It felt surreal. Somehow, through the grace of God, I managed to remain sober.

Remarkably, there was an upside to all of this tragedy: it brought the family even closer together, just when we needed it most.

TOMMY—

After I admitted I needed help, Mom stepped into the kitchen and called Dad at work. "He's ready to get help," she said, unable to hide her relief. She gave him a brief rundown on what'd happened. Just hearing her recount this shit for my dad was embarrassing. Finally, she told him to come home.

My dad showed up a short while later, and we sat in the family room. Mom took the lead. "I think we need to do this now. Strike while the iron's hot."

Everyone agreed.

Mom handed me a sheet of paper with some names and numbers.

"What's this?" I asked.

"Treatment centers. Rehab."

"You want me to call these places?"

"Yes. It's time to take control of your life."

Mom was right, as she often is.

CHAPTER FOUR

TOMMY—

Time is a luxury that allows perspective on stuff that happened to you long ago. A grownup looks back on events with that grownup point of view. When you're still a kid and in the thick of it, those events look completely different.

Things make less sense when you're a child. The stakes seem higher. The hours seem longer, and hope can feel like a distant island you'll never be able to swim to.

Sure, I was twelve years old when I first went to prep school, but the events that unfolded really shaped me and who I was going to become. I know it sounds like bullshit when someone says they remember those days like they happened yesterday. But for me, it's true. I can still see all of it—or most of it, anyway.

I was only starting the sixth grade when I first arrived at the prep school. Unless you're from St. Louis, you haven't heard of this place, so let me give you a little background. It's a private Catholic school for boys that was built in the early 1900s—in other words, from the students' perspective, a ridiculously olden time before anyone could even "like" your shit on social media. The school was started by a priest who founded an order in France, and they practiced a distorted version of these beliefs at the school.

For those who are fortunate enough to go there, the campus itself is a carefully crafted monument to a world of possibility. It's a well-maintained, impressive, old-world monstrosity that makes you feel like you're wandering around a movie set.

What really attracted me to the school was its sports teams. From what I knew, they had the best facilities and coaches, and a great rep for kicking ass when it came to collecting state championships—which they do, way more than your average school. And a ton of NHL players went there as kids.

Naturally, as a huge Blues fan, I was super stoked to be there. But that didn't last long.

On my first day cruising around campus, I felt like a bigger kid. I was excited to be in middle school, thrilled to be somewhere new. I stood a little straighter and walked a little taller. I was desperate to be accepted yet also find some way to stand out. That's a pretty tall order for any twelve-year-old.

I soon learned that the school loved rules almost as much as they loved Jesus. There was a dress code, although thankfully it wasn't too restrictive. We weren't forced to wear some dorky *Dead Poets Society* uniform, with ties and V-neck sweaters. The school kept it simple: collared shirts and khakis with athletic shoes. For some reason, they had this rule that prohibited open-toed shoes. Totally fine by me, since I was never a sandals kind of guy.

The school also had a long list of the kind of rules that cause most students to groan—stuff like a seven-minute maximum for using the bathroom. That seemed kind of weird to me. Isn't it a little excessive to put a time limit on the very human act of using the toilet?

I could just see one of the teachers shouting at me through the bathroom stall door: "Time's up, Mr. Boldt!" What was next? No belches lasting longer than six seconds?

Chapter Four

As time went on, I got used to the school's obsessive rule mentality, however odd it was. But I would never get used to the cruelty of some of the students.

The lay of the land became pretty apparent right off the bat. Many of the kids knew each other from their previous schools. That made me an outsider. I tried to break into some of these cliques, but they weren't interested in new friends.

My twelve-year-old instincts caused me to yearn for attention, for some positive reinforcement. I tried making jokes in class. I tried insinuating myself into conversations. None of the other students would budge. My efforts backfired, with horrible consequences I couldn't have imagined. I was met with immediate ridicule and contempt.

Now don't get me wrong. I'm not looking for sympathy or anything. Lots of kids go through this. Most kids go through this. What most kids don't go through is the nonstop bullying that gradually evolved.

Bullying has been a problem since the dawn of time. It still happens today, and it's not going to stop anytime soon. But these guys at the prep school took it to a whole other level. With them, it became a kind of art form—a sadistic art form. They put a lot of thought and effort into behaving like assholes. It was like they sat around warming their hands by the fires of hell, devising new ways to fuck with me.

Their onslaught started out small, as most bullying onslaughts do. You know: name-calling, shit like that. Remember, I'm not even thirteen years old yet, so I haven't really started any kind of growth spurt. I was kind of on the smallish side, compared with a lot of these other kids. Sometimes these bigger, older kids referred to guys like me as "pencil-neck geeks." Other times, it was a whole lot worse.

It was an all-boys school, so there was a crude fixation on homosexuality. After being there for all of fifteen seconds, you'd figure out the kids considered being gay as the greatest of all possible sins. Labeling another kid "gay" was about the biggest insult you could deliver. Every day, as I would walk the school hallways, I would hear the cruel taunts and shouts.

"Fag!"

"Fairy!"

Other kids would snicker and laugh, and it just kind of snowballed from there. I have no idea how these kids became this way. I can only imagine it was a basic moral failing passed down from their parents.

In my family, we were always taught kindness, respect, and compassion. These characteristics were at the core of who we are and what we stand for. But not these guys. They seemed to delight in being judgmental, hurtful, and just plain mean.

Their ranks grew, as did their efforts to make me miserable. There were about twelve of them, which is a good-size pack to have to deal with and try to avoid on a daily basis. It's no exaggeration to say my life became a living nightmare. No kid should have to go through that.

The verbal assaults were bad enough, but then it started to get physical—and not in the Olivia Newton-John kind of way. I'm talking about violence, flat-out assault.

One time, I was scrubbing the word *faggot* from the door of my locker. They probably could've gotten away with the shorter version, *fag*, but none of these idiots would be singled out for their brains—or their imagination. Defacing school property was right up there when it came to pushing their creative boundaries. These bullies thought writing on my locker was both hilarious and clever, which is probably all you need to know about their collective IQ.

Chapter Four

So there I was, scrubbing away at black marker with a fistful of wet paper towels, as though that would magically take my other problems away with it. It wasn't really working out too well—in fact, it was an exercise in futility, that skill I would come to master a bit later in life.

From behind me came a chorus of laughter, along with a running commentary from the gathered pack of morons cracking jokes that lacked any humor at all. I was doing my best to ignore them because, well, what else was I gonna do? It would be pure suicide to confront all eight of them. They were significantly bigger than I was, which only made things worse.

I was about to give up on this pointless task when a vicious strike caught me right on my tailbone. A kick, I think. Or it might have been a knee.

Regardless, it was totally unexpected. I had no chance to brace for the impact, and let me tell you: that shit really hurt, probably more than you can imagine. A bolt of pain shot up my spine, and my entire body arched forward. I yelped in agony and buckled.

The next thing I knew, I was on the floor. The pain was so overwhelming, my eyes began to tear up. I wanted to get to my feet. I wanted to retaliate. I wanted to say something back. But nothing happened.

Nothing.

The pain was debilitating. The humiliation was too much. The laughter got turned up the dial to eleven, and soon the other students in the hallway were laughing too. There was nowhere for me to hide. All I could do was squirm around on the polished hallway floor, trying to subdue the excruciating feeling. But like the laughter, the pain wouldn't stop.

When I was finally able to sit up, trying to be careful not to make the pain worse, I blinked the tears from my eyes. This only gave them fuel for their insults—the usual moronic names, questioning my sexual orientation and my masculinity in general. Like I said, they weren't the brightest bunch, but brutally effective when it came to the art of bullying.

I found my way to my feet and hobbled down to the teachers' lounge, where I flagged down the closest teacher: one of the priests, dressed in a long black robe like a missionary in some artsy historical foreign film. I want to say his name was Father Chapeau, but that can't be right. *Chapeau* means "hat" in French.

Anyway, Father Chapeau just about shat himself when he saw me. "My goodness, what happened?" he asked.

I reluctantly told him about the attack.

He listened carefully, nodding, occasionally frowning and shaking his head in disapproval. When I was done, he studied me for a long moment like he was drawing deep from his bottomless well of wisdom. "Well, thank you for coming forward and sharing this," he said. "I admire your courage. Your fortitude."

"My what?"

"Your fortitude. Your ability to endure—"

This didn't sound like it was going in the right direction. "Aren't you going to do anything about it?" I asked.

Father Hat seemed put off by the directness of my question, like *Who are you to question my authority?* "Of course. I'll speak with the other students," he said. "This sort of behavior is not acceptable here at our school. Or anywhere else, for that matter."

Even at twelve, I was pretty good at reading people. And I could tell, straight up, that Father Chapeau was full of it. Best of all, he knew that I knew. And he patted me on the shoulder, offered some quote from the Book of Matthew about Jesus turning the other cheek, and sent me on my miserable way.

That was the thing about some of the priests at the prep school: they loved to flaunt their encyclopedic knowledge of the Bible by tossing out some quote that was supposedly relevant to the situation. But how was that actually going to address the problem? Maybe finding some kind of solution would've been nice so that kind of shit didn't keep happening. That was my hope, anyway.

You've got to have dreams, right?

Unfortunately, that's not what happened. What actually happened was a whole lotta nothing. The bullies weren't reprimanded. They weren't disciplined. They probably didn't hear a word about any of it.

If anything, the lack of response from the school encouraged my tormentors. The whole incident emboldened them to step up their campaign of terror on me and other kids they decided were "weak."

Not long after that locker incident, I was out running laps on the track during gym class. It was one of those cold St. Louis mornings when the temperatures hover in the 40s, and an ethereal layer of mist shrouds the ground like some kind of video game, so you half expect an army of zombies to emerge from the fog and come staggering toward you.

If I had my choice that morning, I would've gone with the zombies.

Instead, the bully collective was out in force, yukking it up and looking for ways to mess with my life. One of them—a big lummox of a kid who looked old enough to be in college if he hadn't been held back for his inability to spell *USA*—took me by surprise and shoved me to the ground. He had a good sixty pounds on me, so it wasn't an overly challenging feat for him strength-wise.

Fortunately, I wasn't hurt other than suffering another blow to what little pride I had left. I brushed away the tiny track pebbles embedded in my hands and scraping my knees while the bozos serenaded me with their cruel laughter. Seconds later, I was out of there. But as I passed the bleachers, I was suddenly pelted with droplets of moisture.

WTF?

I stopped in my tracks, confused.

The rest of their posse was perched above, laughing as they showered me in great globs of saliva. They found this shit hilarious, which always baffled me. Who the hell finds this kind of behavior funny? What kind of ass-wipe do you have to be to enjoy the degradation and pain of others?

This is precisely the reason the Incredible Hulk is so popular with kids at that age. You piss off the nerdy little scientist guy, and he turns into a raging, muscle-bound monster who dismantles evildoers and destroys everything in his path.

But as fulfilling as that fantasy might seem to every kid, it almost never happens that way. In real life, the bullies are rewarded. Their shitty behavior is reinforced. There are no checks or balances, and there certainly is no green alter ego to kick their asses. All I could do was go to the gym teacher, Mr. Schlesinger.

Even as I was in the middle of explaining what had happened, I knew Schlesinger wasn't going to do anything about it. I could tell by the smile he fought to suppress and the complete and utter lack of empathy in his ruddy, stone-like face. As far as I could tell, he was one of those guys, a former athlete himself, who wasn't overly sympathetic to the more vulnerable members of the herd. No, he was content to let this "natural selection" play out the way nature had intended, with the weaker falling prey to the stronger. For all I knew, Schlesinger was a guy who might have been a bully himself.

Either way, he did nothing. And nothing changed—except the frequency and intensity of the attacks.

During religion class one day, as I was minding my own business, reading about Jesus and his Bible buddies, this guy hauled off and smacked me—hit me for no reason whatsoever, right out of the blue. After three or four seconds of initial shock, I lost my temper. Without even thinking, I hit him back. And I told him to leave me alone.

The teacher looked up from his own Bible, which was open on the desk before him, and told me to be quiet.

"Me?" I couldn't believe it. "But—"

"Mr. Boldt! That's enough. I won't have you disrupting this class any further."

"Are you fucking kidding me?"

Apparently the f-word was not the proper way to speak to our religious studies teacher. He took great exception to it, along with the other obscenities I strung together in my frustration.

The next thing I knew, it was lunchtime and this guy wouldn't allow me to eat. Instead, I was forced to sit at a long wooden table and write Bible verses in my notebook. It was a pointless, old-timey punishment that would in no way benefit my development as an upstanding member of the Marianist community.

No lunch for you. Now, sit there like some mindless tool and copy words from the Bible into your notebook. That'll teach you.

Teach me what? I'm still trying to figure that one out.

Weekends were different. They offered temporary relief from all that crap—a time for me to hang out with my brothers, play outside in our treehouse, or build stuff like the vintage motorcycles my dad rescued from a scrapyard. We'd work on those bikes, build them together, and learn about mechanics and life in general.

One time I connected a trailer to the John Deere Gator—basically a glorified golf cart–slash–maintenance utility vehicle—and lugged an old couch up onto the flatbed. Then I added a cooler of Mountain Dew and motored around the neighborhood. Some of the other kids jumped aboard; others followed me around like I was the Pied Piper.

Me, being followed by other kids. Can you imagine?

Those were good times with my family and friends. For a brief while, I didn't have to think about the bullies who prowled the halls of my school, bent on destroying me. I didn't have to plan elaborate, inconvenient routes to my classes to avoid their terror. Weekends meant I could be a kid again, free from fear and harm. Then Monday would roll around, and everything would start back up.

I was scared of returning to school, scared of the relentless badgering and pain. It was awful enough to keep me awake at night. And Sundays were usually the worst. Not many kids can fall asleep with that kind of dread consuming their every waking thought. I was no exception.

It's no wonder my mom was willing to do anything to make it stop.

LAURA—

Tommy's problems at school were persistent. It was more than just a few incidents. Tommy was seeing a therapist at this point—a wonderful man named Eric—but the bullying had been going on for a while. There were small acts of humiliation, almost too many to count, like the time they ground handfuls of food in his face. Then there were the truly horrifying attacks, the more aggressive forms of assault. Like when they kicked him in the kidneys and we had to take him to the hospital because he had blood in his urine.

Tom and I did everything we could. We had countless talks with the school, and each time we got the same reassurances, the same promises—and the same disappointing results.

This was painstakingly serious. It was breaking my heart to see Tommy so beside himself, so anxious.

CHAPTER FIVE

LAURA—

How had it come to this? How had this amazing kid of mine, with such a big heart and a bright future, arrived at this terrible place? I knew that he was genetically predisposed to addiction, and that had something to do with it. But there had to be more. What kind of crazy bullshit and sadness happened in Tommy's past that he'd devolved to the point of becoming a bona fide addict?

To shed a little light on this part of the story, let's go back to Tommy at twelve years old—to the time when he first attended that private prep school for boys. A couple of critical events from this time influenced his course in life. I'm sad to say, even though I had my reasons, that I was instrumental in this shift.

I was the one who first gave him a sedative.

I realize that giving my twelve-year-old a Valium doesn't exactly put me in the running for Mom of the Year. I did try calling our family doctor first. He wasn't there, so I left him a message. I wanted to get his opinion. I wasn't being totally irresponsible, after all.

Valium had a different reputation in those days. I was never much of a pill-popper, but back then it seemed everyone had a prescription for Valium or Xanax for some reason. The possibility of addiction never even crossed my mind. Back then, I wasn't sober like I am now. I wasn't a full-blown alcoholic, either—not at that point. A dedicated person in sobriety would never give her child Valium.

Thinking about it now, the fact that Tommy did eventually become an addict makes me wonder if it could have been the Valium or just genetic, if Tommy shared my predisposition just as I shared my mother's. There's no way to be sure what kicked off Tommy's problems with addiction. The Valium seemed liked a good solution in the moment. Even so, it's one I have come to regret. Maybe he plummeted down that rabbit hole just because I did. It makes sense now, having been there myself.

After dealing with my own addiction, I'm aware of the allure—the ease with which you can escape. By numbing yourself with drink—or by placing a single pill in your mouth—you can play that magic Get Out of Hell card.

But Tommy was only twelve years old.

TOMMY—

Things eventually came to a head, of course. The defining moment—the terrible incident that was just too much for a twelve-year-old to handle—happened right outside the school lunchroom.

The prep school served up surprisingly good food: pizza, chicken, sandwiches, fries, a full-on salad bar, even the occasional steak. You could eat whatever you wanted, without limit. This had been one of the big selling points when I first toured the place with my parents. To a ravenous adolescent, this was pure heaven.

So there I was, doing the lunch thing with every other student—the one time we were all in the same place at the same time. The cafeteria was cavernous and always bustling with lively conversation. And there I was, keeping to myself as usual, mowing down a heaping plate of crispy chicken and fries. Across the room, four tables away, was good ol' C. J., basking in the adulation of the other kids.

C. J. wasn't one of the bullies. In fact, he was an old childhood pal. But as luck would have it, he was in the grade ahead of me, so our schedules were different. So even though I had the good fortune of having at least one friend at prep school, that friend wasn't around much. That's why I was pretty much a one-man band.

C. J. was one of those people who seemed to coast through life without a worry in the world. This kid was wise beyond his years and just understood stuff that the rest of us didn't yet. He drank imported water with bubbles and cut his apples into civilized pieces with a small silver knife. He was like the dreamboat character on some sappy TV show, with perfect frosted hair and all the right clothes—the one who's always laughing, always making everyone around him feel better about themselves. Except this wasn't a TV show. It was real. There were no laugh tracks or commercial breaks.

For some reason that defied basic logic, C. J. didn't have to concern himself with the day-to-day shit most of us mere mortals were so stressed about. Nope, not this guy. He had so little drama in his life, it made you scratch your head and wonder about fairness in the grand scheme of the universe. He would somehow emerge unscathed from any confrontation or conflict.

C. J.'s speech carried the trace of some accent that I thought was French but turned out to be Swiss. He was the careful product of years of selective breeding between the uber-rich and the uber-beautiful. His parents were loaded, he was a natural athlete, girls liked him, and the guys wanted to hang with him. All in all, a pretty awesome dude, and someone you'd be pleased to have as a friend and tour guide at a new school.

From all this gushing, you might mistake him for an angel, which he wasn't. Sure, if C. J. had wings, he probably would've taken me under one of them. But even C. J. couldn't ensure that school was all smooth sailing and good times. Even C. J. couldn't make the bullying stop.

I was widely regarded as toxic, so there was no point in joining him at lunchtime. I didn't want to dampen C. J.'s popularity by associating him with someone who fell into the persona non grata category. I didn't want to put our friendship to that test. Maybe I was worried what the outcome might be.

Whatever it was, I left him alone in the cafeteria, unburdened, free to enjoy his perfect existence. All I could do was watch him operate, with just the slightest tinge of envy.

After I finished my lunch that day, I dumped the tray on the stack and meandered toward my next class. Just outside the lunch-room doors, I was once again caught off-guard.

A violent slash whipped across the back of my legs. The pain was so sudden, so intense, it blurred my vision.

I stumbled forward and was met by a human wall that thrust me back with such force, I tripped and almost fell.

Before I could even protest, I was struck again.

Another flash of blinding pain.

I turned to face my attacker: Vince, one of the more vocal members of the bully collective. He grinned as he wound up for another strike. That's when I realized what he had in his hands: a leather belt. He was using it to whip me.

Really?

I was so surprised, I didn't know what to say. Who attacks another kid at school with a leather belt? My brain refused to accept the insanity playing out before me.

Before I could escape, Vince lashed out again. This time the belt struck me in the arm. I howled in pain and twisted away. The other kids cheered in approval.

Soon I was surrounded. My feeble attempts to run were blocked by these larger jeering kids. Vince hit me again and again. Each blow snapped against my body, leaving a fresh welt.

Finally, C. J. stepped into the fray. He grabbed Vince by his arm and pushed him back. "Enough!" he yelled.

The others were startled by his sudden intervention, the loudness of his voice. A few seemed unsure how to respond. Who dared to interrupt their fun?

C. J. stood firm.

For a moment, it could have gone either way. Luckily, the bullies lived up to their reputations as a bunch of chickenshits. After a couple of edgy seconds, they backed down, not wanting to challenge another kid who might actually be capable of defending himself.

Vince pushed his belt back through his pant loops and silently stalked off, pissed that his fun had come to an early end. The crowd dispersed.

Once the threat subsided, C. J. turned to me, his chest rising and falling from the adrenaline pulsing through him. "You okay?" he asked.

"Yeah. Thanks."

"You should report these assholes."

"I already have. A bunch of times."

C. J. looked confused. "Then why—"

"I don't know," I replied. "This happens every day."

He frowned. "From now on, you sit with me. Okay?"

I thanked him, trying to hold back my emotions. I was grateful, but even his friendship was only a small measure of comfort. I still had the rest of the school day to contend with, when C. J. would be gone, and I would be left to fend for myself.

The weekend arrived, and the temporary relief that came with it. That Saturday was spent with my brothers doing brotherly things. I laughed, enjoyed myself, and was able to distract myself from reality—for a little while at least. Then Sunday rolled around, and you know what happened then.

The dread began to creep in.

TOMMY—

It wouldn't be an understatement to say I was freaking out that entire Sunday. At bedtime, it was the usual paralyzing fear of having to go to school the next day. No matter how hard I tried, I couldn't stop thinking about it.

My mom noticed and tried to calm me. Nothing worked. The more we discussed it, the more my anxiety rose. In retrospect, I think I might've actually had some form of PTSD. Who knows? But I did come to learn that all of the bullying was and is certainly a form of trauma.

Soon I was crying.

Mom put her hand on my chest and was mortified. "My God," she said, "your heart's beating a mile a minute." She led me to her bathroom and filled the bath with warm water. Then she had me climb in to try to calm down. It was a thoughtful gesture, but it didn't do much good.

I was tired of pleading, but I asked her again—begged her, really. "Don't send me to school tomorrow." My breathing was shallow and kind of frenzied, like I'd just used the stairs to deliver a dozen pizzas to the top of the Empire State Building.

"Why are you breathing like that, honey?" she asked, keeping her hand on my chest as though she could somehow slow my heart down. She had that look of mom-worry that had become way too familiar recently.

After a few moments, she disappeared. I could hear her making a phone call. Then she came back with something in her hand and a glass of water. "Here," she said as she handed me a small white pill. "Take this."

"What is it?" I asked.

"It's a Valium. It'll help you relax," she replied. "It needs to be swallowed, not eaten."

Since there was no chewing involved, I knew this wasn't your regular kind of pill, and it certainly was no Pez. I popped the pill back, took a deep draw from the water glass, and then wiped my mouth.

My mom sat there expectantly, looking into my eyes.

"It's not working," I said.

"Give it time," she responded with a small mom-kiss to my forehead.

I was about to complain that the pill was a dud when it hit me. A lulling wave of calm rose up and washed over me, the warm caress of a thousand soothing angels.

Wow.

Suddenly, nothing else mattered.

There was no stress. There were no bullies. The entire prep school had been sucked into this dark vortex of euphoria. And that was fine with me.

The world seemed like a different place. A place that was gentle and free from worry. And I wasn't about to complain.

After the bath, I lay down on my bed, and my mom drew the covers up to tuck me in the way only Mom can.

"Get some sleep," she whispered as I drifted off.

And sleep I did, in a profoundly deep, dreamless state where my entire being gave in to emotional exhaustion. It was like the part of the movie when the astronaut drifts away, untethered from the mother ship, slowly orbiting in the blackness of outer space while planet Earth glows in the distance. The audience knows the astronaut is fucked, but he doesn't seem to care. He's content to float off in his space suit, savoring the tranquility of his newfound state of calm.

If you could see inside his space helmet, you would discover a look of serenity on this astronaut's face, a look that says everything will be okay because a new frontier has opened and all of his problems will simply fade away.

Except, of course, they won't.

LAURA—

A little while after I gave the Valium to Tommy, the doctor called back. "That's exactly what I would've done," he said.

Of course, that probably wouldn't fly today. With what we know now about prescription drugs and addiction, I doubt many doctors would be so agreeable. But at the time, our doctor felt it was perfectly reasonable, given the circumstances. And his reassurance made me feel better about my decision.

The Valium, for all its shortcomings, did the trick. And not for one second did I ever imagine it would lead to anything more. I mean, he was twelve, for God's sake! I thought it was a temporary solution, something to help him sleep—something to help him get out from under the suffocating weight of anxiety. Who could have predicted that this first experience would eventually contribute to a full-blown addiction, a ruinous coping mechanism for my sweet, loving, troubled son?

But just seeing him so upset, so completely distraught, made me want to do something. When you see your child crippled with anxiety like that, you feel like you have to do *something*. His little heart was pounding like nothing I'd ever seen before. *Pounding*. I was in sheer agony, watching my son in such pain. I felt like I really needed to try and help.

Who knows? Maybe I gave him the Valium for me.

TOMMY—

Monday rolled around, and I was back at school. Details from the campus seemed a little sharper, the day a little brighter. It was like someone had taken away my fingerprint-smudged sunglasses, and I could actually see the place clearly for the first time.

I thought it was kind of weird, but hey—maybe it was because I'd actually managed to get some sleep the night before. All I knew was, whatever Mom gave me apparently did the trick.

But it wasn't long before that feel-good sensation melted away. The old angst returned as soon as the bully collective noticed my arrival. Fortunately, I was able to dodge them and slip into class without a major incident.

Class started out fine but quickly fell into that horrible, familiar pattern. I had managed to avoid the bullies in the hallway, but this kid named Greeson—a loser with pinched features and a smattering of acne on his mean face—decided to pick up the slack. He was one of the bigger kids at school, clocking in at a good 200-plus. That's a lot for a thirteen-year-old. One look at Greeson, and you could tell he was pretty good with a knife and fork and no stranger to those between-meal snacks.

First Greeson launched into the obvious, unimaginative jabs that bullies tend to rely on—the mindless verbal diarrhea punctuated by the usual name-calling. Then Greeson's friend, another jar-headed fool who looked like the practice dummy for the wrestling team, started laughing like this was the funniest shit he'd ever heard. Like I said, these guys weren't the brightest bulbs in the chandelier.

The teacher, like every other teacher at that place, did nothing. Nada.

Greeson finally quieted, smugly content that he'd delivered his clever and biting insults. That's when, for reasons I can't explain, I decided to fire back. Call it a small act of defiance. Call it suicidal. It doesn't matter. I did it because I had to do something.

Mustering my courage, I said in a loud, clear voice, "Greeson! You're the fattest thing I've ever seen. And I used to work for Greenpeace!"

A few of my classmates laughed. Most were stunned into silence and disbelief. They sat, riveted, waiting for the retaliation that was guaranteed to follow. You don't poke an ape like Greeson and expect no response.

I can still see the smirk vanishing from his bloated face. The shock. The delayed response as the wheels of his feeble mind turned, processing the very notion that he'd been insulted by his victim.

When my insult finally did register, Greeson roared to his feet, uprooting the desk with him. For a second, I thought he was going to fall on his ass. The outrage exploded on his reddened face, the veins in his forehead threatening to burst.

I have to confess: I was scared. I honestly believed this gorilla was going to try to kill me with his bare hands. And all that lay between me and certain death was a frail, seventy-five-year-old teacher who had no intention of wrinkling his pressed shirt.

I was back at that familiar place within the walls of the prep school—alone and threatened. I started eyeing the door, calculating my escape in the few seconds I had left.

Greeson let loose another torrent of deafening insults, like a furious silverback barking at a rival. He did everything but pound his chest.

The teacher reacted at last, sending us both to the principal's office. Jarhead dutifully tagged along, offering Greeson emotional support and promising to kill me at the first opportunity.

"What's this moron paying you?" I asked Jarhead. "I'll double it, and we'll kick the shit out of him."

Neither of them found this particularly amusing.

At the principal's office, I was ushered to a seat and forced to sit down. The door closed. The wall clock ticked louder than I would've imagined, like a school clock in a John Hughes movie.

The principal was one of those collared priests who seemed to believe that all people, regardless of their behavior, are inherently good. While that sounds like an admirable perspective, it's almost always a million miles from the truth. After listening patiently to my account of the situation, and after witnessing firsthand these two morons ganging up on me right there in his office, he offered up another grand platter of bullshit that proved to be just too much.

"You are all the Lord's children," he began. "You were all created in His image. And you all possess that inherent goodness. These disagreements—"

"Disagreements?" I shouted, barely able to contain my disbelief.

"These *disagreements* will subside," the principal continued. "This is only temporary. Like all boys, you blow off steam. You sometimes say things you don't mean to say. You make mistakes. Everyone makes mistakes. And you learn. You grow. You begin to reach the potential that resides in each and every one of you. That is what we believe here at—"

At this point, I stood up.

"Mr. Boldt, I'm not finished."

"No, but I am."

And like that, I turned and walked from the office.

"You're what?" said my mom later as she looked up from her flower arrangement in the kitchen. Having been a career designer, she was good at arranging flowers, selecting the right vase, making it look like the centerpiece in a magazine article.

"I'm done," I said.

Mom was silent. She'd known this was coming. She'd heard it from Eric, my easygoing and strangely cool therapist.

"I'm never going back to that school again," I continued. "I've had it. If you drop me off, I'll leave. These kids are mean, Mom. More than mean. They're evil. And they never stop. I can't take it anymore."

My mom set down her flower clippers, her eyes misty. She knew I was right. This wasn't the first time she'd heard this from me, but I could see that now she suspected it was high time to get me out of that school.

"Okay," she said. "This is St. Louis. We have so many choices for good schools. Let me make some calls."

And that's just what she did.

CHAPTER SIX

LAURA—

The problems at Tommy's prep school had been building for some time, and so had our outrage. The school was not living up to its promise. Tommy and about a dozen other kids were being relentlessly bullied, practically every day. I knew the awful stories Tommy shared with us were just a drop in the bucket. My husband and I were at our wits' end.

We'd talked to the school more times than we could count, informing them again and again. Every time we brought it up, it was always the same empty promise: they assured us it would be dealt with. Action would be taken. The bullies would be disciplined, and Tommy would no longer have to worry. They had this great talent for saying what we wanted to hear. And even after all of that, nothing changed. Just like Tommy, we couldn't take it anymore.

Our frustration was boiling over.

After awhile, we had no choice. We had to get Tommy out of there. It was unhealthy, both physically and mentally. He was heart-broken that he couldn't make friends. The cruelty was devastating. And he was in danger.

It killed me to see him so despondent, like those horrible kids had doused the fire in his spirit. He was so good-natured and kind—the sort of kid who liked hugging people. He was an unusually affectionate kid with an uncommon spark for fun.

Those kids at prep school never gave him a chance. They picked on him because he was an easy target, smaller and weaker than they were. They didn't know who he would grow to become, that he would blossom into a successful athlete.

Tom and I realized we had to get him out of there. His therapist, Eric, wound up championing our cause, which was ironic because he had attended the same prep school himself. We had to find somewhere else where he could flourish. Someplace healthy, where he could realize his potential. Someplace where he could exist without worrying about his very safety.

In retrospect, it seems clear: we should've pulled Tommy out sooner.

TOMMY—

My mom called whoever she had to call, and the next thing I knew, I was enrolled at the local public school: Ladue Middle School.

One condition of me going to this new school was agreeing to an exit interview at the prep school. I certainly wasn't about to argue with that idea. In fact, it sounded powerful, and I was really looking forward to it. I'd be done with that place soon enough. Sharing my reasons for leaving might actually do some good. It was a good process for me, as well as for the next group of kids who were going to be picked on.

As it turned out, a bunch of other students had left for the same reasons. I figured maybe it was time for the priests to reevaluate this inherent-goodness-in-all-kids thing they seemed to be so stuck on.

Unfortunately, the exit interview just echoed the nearly complete lack of accountability from this bunch of somber-faced teachers, expressing their regret with my decision. Even old Schlesinger seemed sad to see me go. The herd was about to thin out a little more. What would the young lions do without easy pickings?

Finally, the principal stood and conceded defeat. "I'm sorry we failed you, Tommy. We did everything we could."

"No, you didn't," said my dad. Then he gestured to the door, and we left.

I was amazed. I'd never seen Dad contradict another grownup like that before, at least not in public. I loved that he had refused to agree with the principal—that both my mom and dad had my back.

Just knowing that I didn't have to go back to that place felt like the biggest relief imaginable. It was this new feeling of freedom, and it might've contributed to some unexpected behavior. No one could've seen this coming, least of all twelve-year-old me.

I began to act out in ways that I hadn't before.

It started out small, like when I decided to take my mom's car for a ride. Naturally, I insisted my eleven-year-old brother Eddy ride shotgun. Never one to say no to a good time, even back then, Eddy hopped into the passenger seat, and we drove off through the neighborhood.

Driving was even more fun than I had imagined, and certainly not as difficult as grownups would lead you to believe. The biggest challenges were ditching the babysitter, pocketing Mom's keys, and steering over the lawn and into the street. After that, we were on Easy Street.

Grand Theft Auto, here we come!

Ol' brother Eddy and I were pretty stoked to be cruising through the neighborhood. We would have made it even farther had the next-door neighbor not spotted us. She just about had an aneurysm when she saw the two of us motoring down the street, barely able to see over the dashboard.

All we could do was smile and wave back.

Less than a week later, I was officially a student at Ladue Middle School. This is an important part in my story for two reasons. First, it was my liberation. I was free from all the restrictions of a private Catholic school. Second, it was the start of my addiction. But we'll get to that in a minute.

So there I was, on the first day of school, strutting the halls and feeling pretty damn good about being there. It was almost like I could hear music that nobody else could hear, kind of like the beginning of that old disco movie with John Travolta where he's bouncing through the neighborhood to some funky Bee Gees song jacked up on the soundtrack. Except I wasn't quite thirteen years old, and I wasn't wearing cheesy, tight disco pants or swinging a bucket of paint.

Ladue was nothing like prep school. In fact, it was like a different world.

As far as campuses go, it was the industrial, nondescript version of a school. Function over form—nothing fancy, nothing historic. Just big-ass brick buildings where kids came to learn or do whatever kids are supposed to do at middle school.

The kids there weren't the same as at prep school, either. In fact, they were just the opposite. There was no pack of sociopathic bullies lurking in the shadows, looking to destroy my life. Everyone was pretty chill. They were curious about me. They wanted to know who the new guy was and why I was transferring then, in the middle of the year.

I was met that morning by a family friend named Kenny, a well-adjusted, bright-eyed kid who seemed to be popular enough.

He introduced me to just about everyone and was excited to have me there. It was nice to be out of the strict environment of the all-boys prep school. No one clocked the minutes on bathroom time. There was no dress code. We were free to make our own disastrous, teenage fashion statements.

Holy shit, what a contrast!

Once I got into it, the classes seemed a little easier, the teachers more relaxed. I started to breathe a little easier, too. In one of my very first classes, this guy named Charlie randomly sat next to me. He wore a faded Aerosmith T-shirt and had this unruly straw-colored nest of hair that probably hadn't seen a comb in years. If he wasn't thirteen, he would've been the kind of guy to have a five-o'clock shadow.

Charlie was a world-class smart ass, and we hit it off instantly. In the middle of the teacher's discussion on American musicians, she mentioned the great Stevie Wonder, and Charlie raised his hand.

"Yes, Charlie?"

"You ever seen Stevie Wonder's band?"

"No, I don't think so," the teacher said.

"Don't feel bad," I said before Charlie had the chance. "Neither has he."

The class broke out in laughter. The teacher said some teacher stuff about interrupting, but neither one of us heard a word of it.

Charlie nodded in acknowledgment. "Good one," he said. "We gonna be friends, or what?"

"Hell, yeah," I responded.

We bumped fists in solidarity. I looked at Charlie with a sly grin, and just like that, we became friends. In fact, we're still friends to this day.

The rest of the school year flew by. I really came into my own and was well liked for the first time in my life. I had friends, the girls started to notice me, and life was good. On the weekends, we'd let loose and have some fun—as much fun as seventh-graders could have. Well, okay, maybe a little more than that. But nothing too crazy.

At first, it was the obvious. You know, whatever beer we could get our hands on—nothing major, nothing a connoisseur would be caught dead indulging. But one thing does lead to another, as the song says.

Drinking became more and more regular when we got together on weekends. In the years to follow, we'd pool our money and load up on Bud Light and Popov—that horrible vodka that costs about twelve dollars a gallon. Popov isn't exactly for the most discerning palate, but it's awesome for teenagers looking to get wasted. In a pinch, it's also good for cleaning paintbrushes.

Through all of this partying, my yearning to be accepted was fulfilled. I was part of the group. I was hanging out with older kids, doing the kinds of stuff they did. I was not ridiculed or judged. I was one of them.

School seemed to take a backseat to the good times. My behavior became worse and worse as time went on. I was more and more disruptive, often disrespectful to the teachers. I fed off the other kids' laughter, their approval. When I think about it now, it's a little embarrassing. I guess you have to chalk it up to my being so young and trying to find my way.

I remember this one kid who wasn't particularly amused with me. Peyton was his name, like the quarterback, and this kid was big—really big. He was athletic, too. And I think he must've been a little jealous of me, for reasons I can only guess. I can still see him staring at me with that menacing glare. Peyton wasn't having whatever I was selling, and that was okay. What wasn't okay was him getting up in my face to make a point of it. It took me back to my days at the prep school.

This scenario was all too familiar. Even though some time had passed, a lot of suppressed emotions rushed to the surface.

To my own surprise, I was more angry than anything. Maybe it's because I took so much shit at the prep school and didn't stick up for myself in the way that I should have. Maybe this was my own Incredible Hulk moment.

"What're you looking at?" Peyton offered. "You little fairy."

"Fairy?" I asked. "I look like a fairy to you?"

He smirked that dumb, bullying smirk, and I knew it had to be wiped from his face.

"Fairy," he said again.

"You think I'm gonna grant you a wish? Make it good, Peyton, 'cause I'm only gonna grant you one. What do you want? Some brains? Or maybe some balls?"

That was all it took for him to charge across the room. In his rage, he lunged. His giant hands opened, ready to throttle my neck. But when I stepped out of his way, his momentum carried him past me and sent him crashing into some chairs. On his way down, I pounced.

This is the part of the story where things aren't entirely clear. An adrenaline rush will do that. I remember straddling this fallen bully and erupting with newfound fury. My anger exploded as a part woke up and screamed to the surface. I was no longer the skinny, geeky scientist.

I was the Hulk.

Peyton blocked the first few, but then I landed punch after

punch. I hit that kid again and again. Each punch was a punch I hadn't thrown in the past.

I'm not sure how long this went on before Charlie and a couple other kids grabbed my arms and pulled me away. I'd like to think it was over pretty quick.

The next thing I knew, I was in the principal's office.

Of course, I was no stranger to this kind of thing. What was new were the circumstances. This time, I was seen as the aggressor. I was seen as the guilty one. Talk about flipping the script.

Peyton, for his part, was banged up pretty good. I said little to defend myself or justify the attack. Instead, I took what the principal was dishing out. As he handed down my sentence, I kept up that detached, hundred-yard stare. When it was all over, I found myself waiting outside the front doors of the school for my mom to come get me.

I was officially suspended. And for reasons that weren't clear at the time, I didn't care. In a weird way, it felt kind of good.

All I could think about was hanging with my friends and getting high.

CHAPTER SEVEN

TOMMY—

Despite the bad habits I was picking up, it's not as though partying and getting in trouble at school were the entire story. Along the way, I also found what seemed like my true calling.

I've always been into sports, and skiing in particular. My parents are avid skiers, and I grew up loving to ski. But the first time I saw people snowboarding, something really clicked.

We were up in Beaver Creek, Colorado, skiing as a family, having a generally awesome time on the slopes. Then I saw them: some kids flying down the mountainside with uncommon grace and agility, like they'd been dispatched by the Greek god of snow. (Not sure he exists, but he should.) But these kids weren't on skis—they were *surfing* down the mountain, all badass. I was mesmerized. If there's such a thing as love at first sight, that was it.

Snowboarding.

Sure, skiing was awesome, but this was a whole other level of awesomeness, and I wanted in. There was something so deeply appealing about the idea of this other sport that I couldn't stop thinking about. Snowboarding was like some crazy-hot girl who had winked at me before turning and walking away.

Wait, what? I was shouting after her. *Where you going? Don't leave! I can change! I can be a snowboarder! Give me a chance, I'll prove it!*

Even at night, my dreams weren't safe. I'd close my eyes and see the slopes, see the rush of the hill as I slalomed my way down at mind-numbing speeds. I'd hear the rhythmic hiss of my board as it sliced through the powder. I could feel the bite of cold as it thrashed my face, reminding me I was alive.

Mom let me take some early lessons, but she wouldn't let me commit. I'm guessing it's because snowboarders had a bad reputation back then. People thought of snowboarders as out-of-control partiers, stoners smoking weed and tearing up ski chalets like rock stars from the 1970s—stuff like that. And some of those beliefs were well-founded, so this stigma followed the sport like an unwanted cloud.

Guys like the legendary Ross Rebagliati didn't help the cause any. As a member of the Canadian Olympic team, he won the gold medal in men's snowboarding giant slalom at the 1998 Games. Later, he tested positive for cannabis and had the medal taken away.

For anyone who knows anything whatsoever about pot, you know that it's *not* a performance-enhancing drug. If anything, it's just the opposite. The fact Ross was able to perform on the world stage and knock out the competition says a lot. The fact he did it with THC pumping through his veins is another story.

Stripping Ross of his medal was a way to set an example for the other aspiring athletes. But the decision was soon overturned, and they gave the medal back.

Huh?

If only the rest of life were that easy.

What was the outcome? Did it serve as a warning to snow-boarders around the world? Hell, no. It made Ross a legend, an icon.

The whole thing helped cement the reputation of snowboarders as weed-smoking daredevils. That might've contributed to my mom's reluctance to let me pursue it.

Aside from this rep for partying, there was the also the assumption that snowboarding was just a more dangerous sport than skiing. And maybe it is somewhat dangerous when you're barreling down a mountain at eye-watering speeds with your feet strapped tightly to a board. But that didn't make it any less appealing.

On a snowboard, I would be in control, taking the mountain by storm, connected on some deeper level that I had never imagined possible. Call it spiritual. Call it metaphysical. Call it what you want. That's how it felt to me.

Snowboarding became my new obsession.

LAURA—

All my boys were great skiers. Tommy was sixth in a national ski race at the tender age of thirteen, before he ever tried snowboarding.

When he started to press for snowboarding, Tom and I had our reservations. Back then, we didn't think of snowboarding as a truly athletic endeavor. In fact, we thought it was just a passing fad. But instead of rushing to judgment, we did what any responsible parents would do before making a final decision: we decided to try it ourselves and see what all the fuss was about.

After some investigating, we signed up for some lessons. We also learned that we would look a little ridiculous if we showed up in our ski clothes. So, in the spirit of learning a new sport (although we weren't even convinced it was an actual sport), we decided to dress the part.

Snowboarding culture was different from the ski culture in many ways. There was much more of a grunge aesthetic, at least back then. The last thing we wanted to do was come off as imposters. So Tom and I showed up in our baggy clothes and flannels, looking like refugees from the Seattle music scene.

Once we hit the slopes, our eyes opened. Snowboarding wasn't quite what we had expected.

We immediately appreciated the athleticism involved, the skills necessary to succeed. And "succeed" at that point meant making it down the slope without crashing and rolling into a frozen ball of embarrassment. No, this wasn't just a sport—it was also an art. Yes, there was a lot more to snowboarding than we had first imagined.

Most important, we really enjoyed ourselves.

As Tom pointed out, though, there was a different attitude among snowboarders. They were more abrupt and carefree than their refined cousins, the skiers. Yet snowboarders also seemed to have a blindside: a predisposition for speed, without the same degree of control.

TOMMY—

Right around the same time as my new obsession for snowboarding was taking root in Beaver Creek, the 2006 Winter Olympics were happening in Italy. Every day, I'd hunker down in front of the TV, arm myself with some basic provisions (soda and chips), and watch as many events as I could.

As I watched, I studied. I made mental notes. The smallest of details were etched in my memory, dominating my thoughts. Later, when I'd close my eyes, it would be like I was still tuned in to the competitors in their races.

At night, I'd lie awake, envisioning myself as part of the American national team. We would travel halfway around the world to represent our country. We'd check in to our rooms in the Olympic Village and goof around in the hallways to blow off steam. We'd get together for team meetings and eat in the cafeteria with the other athletes, even the hockey players.

I could see it all so vividly—see myself racing for the medal, crossing the finish line, raising my arms in victory with tears nearly frozen on my face. Olympic gold . . . I'd worked for it, and it was mine. Even the smallest details from the podium ceremony played out like some carefully choreographed movie I'd written.

Half the time, these visions would bleed into my dreams. It didn't matter. It was all I could think about, whether I was awake or not. Every day it was more of the same. I was glued to the TV, watching the American team compete. And compete they did.

Snowboarder Shaun White was up in the halfpipe, and he was killing it. This was his first Olympics, and he looked totally badass—dressed in white Team USA snow gear and a black helmet, a US flag sewn on his shoulder like a NASA test pilot about to put a new rocket through its paces. I was sold.

If you're not familiar with the term, *halfpipe* isn't a skimpy load of weed in your bong. It's an Olympic-sanctioned snowboarding competition where competitors do incredible tricks in the air while sailing down the course—a huge, semicircular ice ditch with walls taller than your average house. It's kind of like skateboarding, but the faster, more suicidal wintertime version.

Shaun was looking strong that day—not at first, but he came from behind like the sports movie formula: when the underdog dreams of being something, trains his ass off, and takes it all. Only this was the real thing.

His final run was epic—poetry in motion, as they say. This guy wasn't bothered by stuff like gravity, fear, or the physical limits of mere mortals. Shaun was literally flying, and it paid off. After his final midair trick, he touched back down to earth, and he *knew*. He knew he had done what he needed to do. He pumped his fist in celebration and raised his board in salute.

The gold medal was his.

Americans who had made the trip to Turin cheered him on. Draped in an American flag, his shaggy red hair half covering his face, Shaun stood atop the podium. He was all smiles, happily yelling back to the crowd. They loved him. He was the best of the best, representing America.

A dream come true.

The whole thing was pretty spectacular, even from thousands of miles away in the comfort of our family room. I was completely mesmerized. I didn't even realize my dad was standing behind me, watching the ceremony.

"Pretty cool, huh?" I heard him say.

"Yeah, that guy's awesome," I said without moving my eyes from the TV.

We watched together in silence for a little longer. They played Shaun's gold medal run again, slowing it down so it looked like a 7UP commercial.

Prying my eyes from the TV, I turned to my dad and said, "What do you think?"

I could tell by the look on his face that Dad wasn't too keen. We were a family of skiers, after all. He shared a bunch of reasons that I shouldn't switch to this new sport, but I was relentless.

I began to pace the living room, making my case like a teenage lawyer before the jury. Finally, with my closing arguments firmly stated, I awaited the verdict.

Dad was taking his time and seemed to be thinking it over. When I was about to launch into it again, he finally responded, "Tell you what. Let's suit up and hit the slopes. You beat me in a race, you can snowboard."

At first I thought he was joking. But no, he was serious. This was a challenge. A challenge I was up to.

As I dragged on my ski clothes, I imagined myself as that underdog in the movie. I had prepared for this day, when I would prove to the world that I was not a joke or a loser. Things were looking impossible, and I had suffered a whole bunch of setbacks. People around me didn't believe I would ever win. But I was the hero, and I was going to pull it off. I was Shaun White. I was going to win this race.

Who doesn't imagine themselves the underdog who triumphs against all odds? But that's not always how it plays out in the movie called life.

My dad took me up to the race course at Beaver Creek, which snakes down the face of a steep mountain. It looks pretty awesome, even from a distance. The way it works is this: you pay fifteen bucks, and you can use this totally professional race course. You can compete against the other guy using the clock like they do at the Olympics, or you can race two different tracks, head to head.

My dad and I agreed that racing head to head was the way to go.

There was something pretty exciting about racing next to the guy who'd taught me pretty much everything I knew. It was like an Xbox game, except we were actually out there in the real world doing it, and not sitting in someone's basement with a mouthful of Cheetos.

So there we were, at the top of the run, the tips of our skis hanging off the edge of this steep-as-hell mountain. The red-faced resort employee in a snowsuit got all serious and began to count down like it was New Year's Eve: "Seven, six, five, four, three, two . . . Go!"

I pushed off, and so did my father.

The pitch was steep. It took a few milliseconds to gain momentum and get up to speed, but then . . . *boom*! We were flying. Gravity did its thing, and I did my best to help it. We were accelerating down that hill at a sick speed. Flags marking the course flew past in a blink.

Dad was ahead at first. I didn't really look over, but I could see him at the periphery. Each hard turn he made sent up a shower of snow spray.

I tucked into every corner, slicing into the powder, coming out of the turns with practiced precision. This was my chance, and I wasn't going to blow it.

The cold felt invigorating on my face. The mountain reminded me I was alive. The world came at me with unnatural speed. The course blurred past. Out there on the slope, I was in my element: no school bullshit, no bullies, no nothing. Just pure adrenaline.

Just me, the mountain, and my father.

As we zigzagged down that course, I began to overtake him.

Dad doubled down. He was super competitive and not about to let his teenage son beat him. Instead, he pushed me. This wasn't going to be a free ride. He tested my limits, my ability to compete for something I truly wanted.

In the final stretch, I tucked down, skis together, poles under my arms.

I crossed the finish line a heartbeat before he did.

I stood in victory, slowing myself, the skis riding rough over the grooves at the bottom of the run. The sun felt warm on my face.

Still in a haze of shock, I didn't quite celebrate Shaun White–style, but I felt pretty good. I had pulled it off.

Somewhere on the slopes, someone cheered. I wasn't sure if it was for me, but what the hell. I liked the sound of it. It was exciting, especially for a thirteen-year-old.

My dad, to his credit, laughed. "Congratulations," he said as he raised his tinted ski goggles. "That was one hell of a race. You did it." Dad grinned, appreciating the moment.

And that was it.

True to his word, Dad bought me the gear to start snowboarding.

If you're not a typical gearhead, know this: gear is always exciting. It helps you visualize your goals, to see them unfold in the movie that is your imagination. Perhaps it's the newness, the promise of greatness and achievement. It's the tangible, physical thing that makes you realize what's possible, that really makes you want to get out there and hit the slopes. That's the thing about gear: it gets you dreaming.

Will those dreams become reality?

Will you become better, faster, ready for anything?

I wanted to find out.

So, there we were, Dad and me, in the local snowboard shop not far from the mountain. We started with the obvious choice: a proper snowboard. Prowling the aisles of the snowboarding shop, one particular Burton board caught my attention. They called it a Punch, and this one was grey with these wicked skulls on it. Even the logo looked cool: a skull and crossbones where the *O* in *Burton* should have been.

It was totally badass. I knew I had to have it. My teenage self couldn't resist. (This trait would eventually lead to other problems.)

Fortunately, Dad agreed.

The guy at the shop helped outfit me with boots, bindings, and a new suit to get down the mountain in style. The suit choice was easy: snow white, like Shaun White's Olympic get-up. If I was going to be the best, I might as well dress like it.

With all my new gear packed into my dad's car, I was pumped with anticipation. We couldn't get back to the mountain fast enough.

It wasn't long before I had my first run down the slopes in my own gear. Riding that board made me feel like the outlaw version of the Silver Surfer—ready to tackle the slopes, outdo the bad guys, or take on whatever else the world threw at me. It wasn't long before I realized I was getting the hang of it.

I dove into the sport with the kind of commitment usually reserved for Kool-Aid–drinking cults. And unlike those poor fuckers who wound up facedown on the jungle floor, this shit started to click for me.

My hunch was right. This was my calling.

Snowboarding came to me naturally. It became my life, a literal extension of me and who I was.

Was this another aspect of my addictive personality? Maybe.

Was it healthier than drugs and alcohol? Shit, yeah.

Did I approach it with the same kind of vigor and commitment? I'll keep going with the story, and you tell me.

LAURA—

Tommy was taking his new sport so seriously that Tom and I decided to find him a qualified snowboarding coach. We looked at a number of candidates, but the answer to our search turned out to be a great guy named Dave Piket.

Dave is a former Olympic skier who represented Canada in

competition. He was gifted, patient, and an enormously positive influence on Tommy, and all our boys for that matter. Not only did he teach Tommy that he could win, but he also instilled in him a sense of self-worth. We couldn't have asked for more.

This is what the serious athletes did, and we wanted nothing less for our son. We wanted to steer Tommy toward a more disciplined approach to the sport—and away from some of his daredevil antics.

CHAPTER EIGHT

TOMMY—

Forgive me if this sounds arrogant, but I was kicking ass on the mountain. People around me began to talk about the promise I was showing. So I entered NASTAR—the National Standard Race—and suddenly I was a teenaged competitive snowboarder.

NASTAR is the biggest such race program in the world. It allows skiers and snowboarders of all ages and abilities to compete with one another, and even to measure up against national champions, regardless of where they are. Since it started back in the late 1960s, more than six million people have participated. I thought it was also kind of cool that several US national ski team superstars first came to notice through NASTAR.

Each NASTAR course is basically a modified giant slalom course with a dozen or more gates that each racer has to maneuver. A bunch more rules help standardize these courses from one resort to the next. I was going to be tested against the best.

You get the appeal. *Any cocky teenage athlete who's coming into his own has to figure: Why not? What have I got to lose? Why not test myself against everyone else, even the big dogs?*

A big snowboarding race was coming up at a NASTAR course

in Park City, Utah. What better way to put all my hard work to the test?

My brother Eddy, who was also an awesome skier, decided he'd put himself on the line to see how he'd measure up. Our little brother Peter, an equally amazing skier, also competed. We had never raced on this level before, and I have to confess: I was more than a little nervous.

I wasn't worried about wiping out and eating a face full of snow. No, that part I could live with. I was more nervous to discover I might not be as good as people were saying. Deep down, I knew that wasn't the case, but it does kind of weigh on you. It's that nagging feeling: *What if I'm not quite as good as I think?*

If it were true about me, that shit would go over like a lead badminton birdie. But I figured there was only one way to find out. I had to do it. Measure up or shut up.

Then there was the waiting, counting down each day like a seven-year-old staring at a Christmas calendar. But like Christmas morning, it finally arrived.

Race day.

It was one of those amazing, clear days when the sun beats down on the mountainside and warms the air, creating one of those scenarios every skier dreams about. Everything was so perfect, it was surreal.

The Park City race course was packed. Family and friends crowded nearby to offer encouragement and enjoy a good old excuse to just have fun together. I kept thinking about my brother Eddy and wanting to wish him luck.

Where is he? I scanned the crowd of faces but didn't see him. I couldn't find him on any of the designated race slopes, either, so I figured he must have already raced.

Coach Piket was there—one of my all-time favorite exports

from the Great White North. True to his reputation, he was focused on keeping me calm, keeping my thoughts on the race before me. Probably better than anyone, he knew what this race could potentially mean for me.

Coach Piket went into detail about the slalom flags: how each one was spaced differently, adding to the challenge of the run. He talked me through the course from memory—strategizing, planning when to initiate each turn on each flag, hoping to give me that extra edge. He reminded me about the importance of body positioning.

I listened in agreement, feeling as ready as I ever would be. Coach Piket knew what he was doing, drawing from a wealth of experience as an amazing skier and an Olympic athlete. Yet for some reason, I couldn't stop thinking about Eddy.

Where is he?

My dad asked, "What's the matter?"

"Nothing," I replied. "Just trying to find Eddy."

My dad hesitated. "He already raced."

"Oh. No one told me."

"You focus on your run. We'll find Eddy after."

"How'd he do?"

Dad hesitated again.

It was super weird. Was he hiding something from me?

"He's fine," Dad said at last.

Exasperated, I said, "I didn't ask how he's doing. I asked how he did. In his race. What was his time?"

Again, Dad shrugged it off without giving me a straight answer. I thought something might be up, but I had nothing more to go on in the Case of the Mysterious Disappearing Eddy. Besides, it was time to line up for my own race.

This was a little different than racing my dad. There was a greater sense of seriousness, like I was trying to really prove something with a bunch of people watching, looking entirely unimpressed, waiting for me to blow it.

I pulled up to the start gate, snapped into my bindings, and waited until they called my name. It seemed like it took about twenty hours.

Waiting for a race is about as fun as watching paint dry. What was taking so long? Was this part of some conspiracy to throw me off my game? Were they making more snow? Was Domino's late in delivering lunch? What was going on?

Luckily, Coach Piket was there, steadfast as always—the encouraging, calming force.

Finally, I heard the words I'd been eagerly waiting on: "Tommy Boldt. You're up!"

My heart lurched. I felt like a hospital patient getting the shock paddles. I heard my pulse drumming in my ears and took a few deep breaths. Then Coach Piket and I tapped fists.

"Go get 'em," he said.

"Aren't you going to wish me luck?" I asked.

"You don't need it," he smirked with confidence.

I stood there waiting, ready to prove myself. Time seemed to slow. My heart settled, almost back to normal. The crowd faded. I could hear the distant whisper of the wind in the trees.

The phrase *maximum entropy* crossed my mind, though I'm still not exactly sure what that means—something about choosing what is best from a number of possibilities. It was time to channel my positive energy, get my head in the race, and choose the perfect range and points when calculating my turns and my speed.

Someone, somewhere, laughed in counterpoint to this new state of tranquility, breaking the spell. I bent down, put my gloved hands on the two yellow starter blocks on either side of me, and waited. My hands tightened on the blocks, waiting for the command to propel myself forward.

And then it came . . .

"Go!"

I pushed off with all my strength, plummeting down that mountain at two and a half times the speed of sound. (Okay, maybe I'm exaggerating a little. I'm prone to doing that every once in a while.) But there I was, hurtling down the mountain, arms out to balance myself like the Silver Surfer, riding my board to the extreme, a hair away from wiping out . . .

But, no! I kept going.

A blur of orange whipped by as I passed more safety fencing. I was in the zone, running the gauntlet, flags snapping past so quickly, I barely saw them. I took each turn and cut back hard, narrowly missing the flagged poles that marked the course. I was on such an extreme angle that my elbow and knee were almost touching the packed snow.

It's pretty amazing what you can pull off when you decide the laws of gravity don't apply to you.

Almost at the end of the run, my board cut the ice and snow with a sharp hiss. I was in control—complete and utter control. And it was beautiful. I was so focused that nothing else even entered my thoughts. It was just me and the mountain, having it out.

And before I knew it, I was done. I crossed the finish line. The race was over.

I returned to a standing position and slowed to a stop before unclipping my first boot and stepping onto the hard-packed snow. I looked around, but after a few encouraging cheers, people turned their attention to the next racer.

I had no way of figuring out how I'd done. And to my surprise, I wasn't that bothered by it. I had done what I came to do. I was happy with my performance. I had done my best. Now it was out of my hands.

But I still felt this urgent need to find Eddy. And once I tracked down my dad, he confessed what he had been holding back.

Eddy was in the hospital.

LAURA—

Eddy's accident was one of those truly horrifying things you never want to see happen, especially to your own son at thirteen years old, or any age for that matter. And I saw much of it unfold, even though Peter was racing at the same time.

I loved watching my boys compete, being there to offer them my support. I attended most of the races my kids entered, happily helping out wherever I could. Usually this would entail me skiing down to the bottom of the run, holding my sons' overclothes while they raced.

Over the years, I've spent a lot of time waiting at the bottom of a lot of runs. More often than not, I'd settle into a familiar routine. This would give me time to socialize with the families of other competitors, and there was a sense of camaraderie. Tom, on the other hand, preferred to be with the boys at the top of the run, focused on their race and whatever they needed beforehand. I'd communicate with Tom or the coach through a walkie-talkie so we could coordinate our efforts.

When I reached the bottom of the hill that day, before Eddy came down his run, I noticed some of the other racers struggling with the icy conditions. I called back up to warn Coach Piket.

"You're going to have to sharpen his skis," I said over the walkie-talkie.

And like any good coach, that's precisely what he did.

Nobody was at fault. We did what we felt was in the best interest of Eddy winning his race.

He started off with an impressive run, too. After six or seven gates, he went into a hard turn, and his binding broke. The ski went flying into the air and came down, slicing into his leg. It was a freak accident.

My instincts took over. I handed Billy, who was maybe two or three years old at the time, to one of the other parents. Then I ran up the hill to Eddy.

Tom was already skiing down from the top of the mountain, but he was a few minutes away. It felt like there wasn't a second to lose—not with Eddy lying in the snow, bleeding like that.

I still remember charging up that steep hill, focused, determined to get to my son. I was used to exercising at that altitude, so I wasn't hampered by the steep incline. As I ran, the course announcer came over the PA system. "I assume you're the mom," he said, for all to hear. "We need you to get off the course! Now!"

"I assume you're not a mom!" I shouted back as I kept my pace up the slope. "If you were, you wouldn't be telling me to get off the course!"

"You need to get off the course immediately!" he said. "Ski Patrol is on the way!"

I could see the red and white crosses on the jackets of two men hurrying to the accident scene—to my boy. Still, I kept running up that mountain, supercharged with worry.

Ski Patrol did manage to get there a full minute ahead of me. They were already loading Eddy into "the basket," a stretcher for injured skiers. I had always called it "the casket," though, and the very sight of it made me exceedingly nervous, especially with my son loaded inside, covered in his own blood.

Tom arrived into the chaos moments later, and we were all huddled over Eddy. He had been smart enough to shed his racing bib and use it as a tourniquet to stem the flow of blood. Even so, there was a sense of urgency to get him medical attention at the resort.

We went down to the resort's triage at the bottom of the mountain, and minutes later, I went with Eddy in the ambulance to the hospital. Tom stayed behind with Billy to collect Tommy and Peter after their races.

"Can you feel your fingers and toes?" I asked over the shoulders of the paramedics who hovered above him. I was terrified that he might have some sort of nerve damage.

"Mom, I'm fine." Typical Eddy.

Despite the horrific blood-soaked scene, he was calm and okay. Thank God! And I had to admit, hearing him downplay the accident made me feel a tiny bit better.

TOMMY—

One look at Eddy in his f'd-up state, and you'd think he'd been on the losing end of a swordfight with a master samurai. And I wouldn't blame you. Except the cut had come from one of his skis.

A lot of people don't know this, but racers will sharpen their skis to a finely honed, razor-like edge. It allows them to really bite down through the ice and snow, giving skiers greater control over the madness while shaving seconds off their performance.

The problem is, skis that sharp can also shave the flesh off your limbs.

Chapter Eight

When Eddy took a sharp turn on his qualifying run, his ski popped free and flew into the air. He wiped out, of course, and that ski sliced right through his ski pants, nearly severing his leg. It was a one-in-a-million type of accident.

As you'd probably guess, this was not a pretty sight. My mom was clearly upset. Dad had explained it all to me as we hurried off the mountain and fired up the car, but hearing Mom describe the events that led up to the accident was far more entertaining. She has always been a great storyteller.

I may have been the kid who just sped through a NASTAR race, but I had nothing on my dad as he drove to the hospital like a NASCAR racer. Within minutes, I was in the recovery room with Eddy and the rest of my family.

Eddy smiled when he recognized me. "Hey, what's up?" he asked, his voice weak.

I could tell he was on some kind of pain medication, and rightly so. When that shit is used for its intended purpose, it can work wonders.

He was holding an imaginary machine gun and making gun noises with his mouth—you know, that *rat-tat-tat* noise teenage boys love almost as much as the sweet sound of flatulence. He was in his own first-person shooter game, like he'd jumped inside an Xbox and was the hero of *Call of Duty* or something. Yes, Eddy appeared to be having a good old time.

"How're you doing?" I asked.

"Oh, you know," Eddy replied. "Scraped my leg pretty bad."

"Scraped?"

I could tell by Mom's face that this was a classic example of Eddy-style understatement. He wasn't just scraped up. He'd severed two arteries in his leg—a wound so serious, it required 98 stitches and staples. The gash went all the way to the bone, from midthigh to below his knee, extending almost to his calf. The surgeons had to do layers of stitches and staples, both internal and external. That sure was a lot of operating room for a "scrape."

Coach Piket finally arrived, and he pulled me aside. After the race he had caught up with me, excited and eagerly awaiting the results. Maybe it was his Canadian intuition, or maybe one of the race officials tipped him off. Or maybe he just sensed I'd done well.

Now I would find out.

"You won," he said simply.

I was stunned. "The race?"

"No, an award for asking silly questions." He grinned that awesome, proud-coach grin, and then he gave me a hug. "You did it."

Coach Piket had looked up the results online before coming over to deliver the news. My family couldn't have been happier. Even Eddy, in his justifiably sedated state of mind, took a break from shooting nonexistent bad guys and gave me a thumbs-up.

I won.

I *came in first.*

It took awhile to set in, especially with all of us more concerned about my brother, even though he seemed to be recuperating nicely. Eddy appears to have gotten that superhero gene from Mom—the one that gives you a sunny disposition and a ridiculously speedy recovery. In no time, still looped on painkillers, he was messing around in a hospital wheelchair.

Being the caring brother I am, I couldn't allow him to have all this fun alone. No, sir! I did what any good brother would do. I joined him.

The two of us raced around the room in dueling wheelchairs,

banging into each other like finalists at a smash-up derby. Not to be left out of the fun, Peter found his own wheelchair and was soon crashing into just about everything in his path.

We did wheelies, knocking into stuff and creating mild havoc, to the chagrin of the unimpressed hospital staff. Mom and Dad weren't sure what to make of it, but they were happy to see their boys return to form.

Mom finally put the kibosh on the whole thing, saying, "We've had enough injuries for one day."

The next day, there was an awards ceremony at the race course. Having won in my age division, I stepped up to the podium to receive my medal. Peter, eleven at the time, won third place in his division that year too. It was an impressive run. We were all proud of him, and it gave us yet another reason to celebrate.

To my surprise, Eddy was released from the hospital and made it to the ceremony. Bundled up against the cold and balancing on crutches, he was there along with the rest of the family, cheering me on. Looking back on it now, I realize how much that meant to me. The whole thing was pretty emotional, and it was a huge relief to see my brother looking better in such a short time.

Family dinner that night was at a local restaurant not far from the hotel. Nothing fancy: a burger-and-pizza kind of place, served by waiters with name tags who felt compelled to introduce themselves at the table. We ordered a round of sodas, not the kind of scientifically tested nutritious intake today's athletes consume. Eddy seemed to be doing great despite his injuries. His appetite certainly hadn't suffered after his surgery. His burger and fries didn't stand a chance.

The following day came the Race of Champions, and it doesn't take a scientist to figure out what that entailed: a competition between all gold medal winners in all snowboarding age groups. I'd get to compete against racers way older and more experienced than me. I didn't know it then, but many of them would later go on to be my teammates.

I was up and at it, bright and early. A lot of times, it's hard to sleep the night before a big race. But I hit the course well rested and feeling ready. Everyone was excited for me to compete on an even larger scale—especially me.

Coach Piket was there, providing guidance and generally doing a great job of keeping me focused. He may have been more excited than anyone.

I'll spare you the details of the race, but I will tell you it was one of my better efforts. When they announced the results, to everyone's amazement, I had finished second overall—ahead of racers a whole lot older and more experienced than I was. Sure, it was handicapped, but it was still a fully awesome experience.

Once again, I had taken the challenging course with a confidence and aggression that bordered on insane. I didn't care who I was racing or how much older they were. I knew deep down that I could do it. I could show everyone. And I did.

LAURA—

When Tommy competed in the Race of Champions and finished second overall, I knew it was a truly impressive feat. To put things in perspective, the racer who won gold was fifty-five years old and a former Olympic skier. Tommy was all of fourteen years old and managed to come pretty close. Nothing made me happier than seeing Tommy on the podium, being rewarded for his performance.

He was still so young—not even close to being full grown. When he won the gold, he climbed onto the podium in front of everyone, wearing those baggy pants that were so popular in those days. His pants were falling down, and you could see the tops of his plaid boxers.

I loved it. It was so hilarious—so Tommy.

The guy who won silver that first day was still taller than Tommy, even though Tommy was standing on the podium. It was especially wonderful because it reinforced how incredible it was that Tommy had won.

In the context of his life, snowboarding was an important undertaking. At the time, he was still reeling from the horrors of the prep school, with all of its bullying and other nonsense. He was surrounded by so many people telling him he couldn't do this and couldn't do that. I think all of that fueled some of his motivation to pursue snowboarding. It was his own sport, unlike skiing. That might have been part of the attraction. Snowboarding allowed him to forge his own way, his own identity, his own path to success.

Tommy has always been a unique individual, an uncommon spirit. This exciting pursuit allowed him to fully express himself in a frontier of the unknown. It opened up challenges that seemed daunting yet somehow within his reach.

I didn't realize this at the time, but it's clear to me now—the hindsight thing again. I don't know why we didn't honor his pursuit of snowboarding in the very beginning. I don't know why we didn't trust what he wanted, as it proved to be such an incredible experience and an opportunity for success on so many levels.

I guess it's a natural tendency to lump all of your kids into the same category. But Tommy's a circle, and he's not going to fit into a square, no matter how hard anyone tries—including his parents. And why should he?

One of the last things Charlotte ever said to me was just that: I should honor Tommy. She stressed his individuality, his one-of-a-kind spirit. She urged me to embrace him and not try to change him. And she was right. My son deserved to be honored for who he is.

CHAPTER NINE

TOMMY—

After I stepped down from the Race of Champions podium, a guy approached me. There were a lot of people there that day. I was surrounded. People were congratulating me. Friends were happy for me. Even total strangers and a handful of cute girls, which was perfect in its own way. But this one guy stood out.

He was soft-spoken, with a calm disposition and a contagious smile. You could tell he was one of those super cool dads to some lucky grown-up kids. He couldn't have been nicer.

"You have a true talent," he said. "Especially for someone your age."

"Thanks," I replied, wondering where this was going.

He told me that he owned a small shop not far from the resort—a snowboard shop. "I'd like to sponsor you for next season," he said.

I know it's kind of a cliché to say, *My jaw dropped*. But in this case, it was true.

The guy handed me his business card. I was stunned. I couldn't believe what I was hearing.

This was it. The next step. A sponsorship to help get my name out there.

"You raced really well," he continued. "It'd be nice to see what you could do with some pro race boots and a race board. Come by this week, I'll set you up. Get you properly outfitted. No cost to you or your family."

His generosity hit me like a pine branch to the forehead—totally unexpected. It took me a minute to find the right words.

"Wow, thank you. That's awesome."

We shook hands, and the guy told me he was at the shop every day except Saturdays and Sundays. As he slipped back into the crowd, he said he was looking forward to seeing me again soon.

I stuffed his card into my jacket pocket, but when I got back to my room later, it wasn't there. And for the life of me, I couldn't remember the guy's name.

I searched everywhere, frantic, desperate to find this card—a behavior that would later return when I scrounged for missing pills or a trace of cocaine residue from the night before. Even after turning my hotel room upside down, there was still no card.

I thought about returning to the course, but it was already dark outside. Snow had started to fall.

I was pissed. I sank down onto the hotel bed, slumping back in defeat. What had started out to be a gearhead's dream turned into a nightmare of epic proportions. It was such a gut-wrenching tease: high-end professional gear provided to me free of charge by some too-cool-to-be-true stranger, and now it would never happen.

Maybe that's just what it was: too cool to be true.

Thankfully, I had other things in life to be grateful for. The following year, I won the national championship in snowboarding and further established myself in the NASTAR racing world. The year after that brought more of the same when I took second overall. I continued to do well on the national stage, and there was talk of me advancing even further.

But I just felt so bad. This guy had recognized something in me and was prepared to back me. And for all he knew, I blew him off without the decency of even a courtesy phone call. This bothered me more than losing all the free pro gear.

Even though it was an honest mistake, I was destined to be dismissed as some ungrateful punk. It haunted me.

I loved snowboarding, and I loved competing. I was good at it, and there seemed to be a real future ahead for me. Not many teenagers get to experience that. I was one of the fortunate few.

But something happened after I turned fifteen and headed into freshman year. As I reflect on this now, it's hard to put down in words. Things just . . . changed.

It's kind of strange to even admit it, but my enthusiasm for snowboarding began to fade. Suddenly, it didn't provide the same rush. It didn't give me the same sense of accomplishment. Races weren't nearly as satisfying, and the training felt more like work than it had before. I was changing and didn't even realize it.

While this transformation was unfolding, Coach Piket moved back to Canada because he couldn't get his visa renewed. I can't say it was a huge surprise, because I knew he was struggling with that issue. Still, it kind of threw a wet blanket on my already fragile enthusiasm.

Not long after that, I quit competing altogether. This coincided with me starting to smoke weed and drink, though it's probably no coincidence. Without snowboarding to get me high, I needed something else in my life to take its place.

Drugs and alcohol seemed to fit the bill.

That summer, I figured I needed something—anything—to

serve as a replacement for the grip snowboarding used to have on me. The drugs and alcohol were taking their share of my time and attention, but I needed another physical outlet, another sport. Something I was good at.

Xbox was a serious contender, but no matter how hard I tried to convince myself, playing *Call of Duty* didn't offer the same physical benefits as actually getting off my ass and doing something. There also wasn't a particularly bright future in playing video games, at least not for most people. It probably would be a lot tougher to get a scholarship somewhere as an ace Xbox competitor than as an actual athlete who broke a real sweat.

That left tennis. It was another passion of mine, and I decided to dedicate myself to it the way I had with snowboarding.

When I was at Ladue, I played in USTA tournaments separately from the school, and I'd put up some pretty good numbers. One day Coach Theo, who was also the high school tennis coach, asked me to come hit some balls. I met him the next morning on the court, and we went at it. It was a spirited workout, hitting back and forth. I think Coach Theo was impressed that I could keep pace with him and match his intensity, even though I wasn't even in high school yet.

"You should try out for the team," he said between strokes.

I made the varsity team in my freshman year of high school. Coach Theo put me in doubles, and it was great. I dove into tennis with the same commitment I'd given snowboarding.

At the not-so-tender age of fifteen, I was in the best shape of my life. I could go forever without getting tired. I'd be the first person on the court at practice and the last one to leave at the end of the day. I'm pretty sure that won me favor with the coach and the rest of the team.

I'd use the ball machine to work on my backhand, my forehand, all my hands. I'd fill a shopping cart with tennis balls and hit 300 serves in a row. When it was over, I'd collect the balls and do it all again. At that stage in my development, I had it in my head that the more balls I hit, the better I would become. After three shopping carts' worth, I had to be approaching peak form.

Tennis was it for me. I loved the challenge. I loved the relentless pace. Breaking a sweat was harder back then. By the end of practice, I'd left it all on the court and was completely exhausted.

My doubles partner on the team was the incomparable Roscoe Beauregard. By incomparable, I mean that rare guy who did not look at all like an athlete. If someone told you he was the head food taster for Krispy Kreme, you'd believe it. Roscoe was this big, beefy dude who looked like he'd get winded climbing the ladder to a diving board.

When Roscoe and I stood next to each other, we looked like the number 10. I wouldn't say he was actually fat, at least not in a Chris Farley kind of way, but he was definitely short for his weight. And like the amazing Chris Farley, Roscoe had a gift for making people laugh. That went a long way when we had to travel for tournaments.

On the court, he was no slouch, either. For a big guy, he could cover ground as well as anyone. I think that surprised a lot of people, especially the players we competed against. Having a partner like that was an awesome tactic, too. Other players would be quick to dismiss us. Then we'd deliver an ass-kicking and have the last laugh. Old Roscoe could really hit the hell out of the ball.

In no time, tennis became the new snowboarding for me, and I loved it. I was thrilled to find another sport that I seemed to excel at. Rod Laver was my role model. He was old school—not exactly among the most popular players of our time. But I loved that he was a lefty like me. Plus, he had some awfully cool shoes from Adidas.

I started to fantasize that maybe Adidas would one day design shoes for me: *The Adidas Tommy Boldt. Now with hidden compartment for all your recreational drug needs.*

On the court, my weapon of choice was a Babolat racquet, which apparently maximized the strength of your return by its sheer design. Whatever its secret was, it did the job, giving off that big, meaty *thwop* whenever I hit the ball.

And as with snowboarding, I dressed the part. I wore Fila shorts and shirts like another tennis idol, Björn Borg, except mine were more urban than Swedish, with a bold mix of orange, blue, and black.

I worked hard to refine my game, spending countless hours refining my serve, my ground strokes. Coach Theo showed little mercy as he put us through our paces. I became better and better, and enjoyed being a part of another team, another group.

My days on the court, running never-ending drills, did wonders for my fitness, taking it to another level. I got off on pushing my physical limits, working up a sweat, and never wearing out. If done right, playing tennis can be a real workout. If done right, the endorphins can get you high.

For a while, this became my new addiction. But as with snowboarding, there was competition for my attention. I also enjoyed my time away from the court. Good times were everywhere I turned, and at that age, it was hard to say no. I'm not making some kind of lame excuse; my choices were mine all along. But temptations are hard to resist when you're a teenager, particularly when all your other friends are having such a good time.

My days on the varsity tennis team came to a rather abrupt

finish. It was the end of a good first season. We were at a tournament in some nameless town, playing against another high school team. Roscoe and I had finished our match, and I was busy packing up, zipping the cover back on my racquet.

Coach Theo noticed and asked me what I was doing.

"Putting my stuff away," I said, without giving it much thought.

"We're not finished," he said. One of my teammates hadn't finished his match yet.

"I'm done," I responded as I stuffed my towels into my bag.

"Tommy, you know the rules. No one leaves until everyone's played. You need to be on the team bus."

I shrugged and hefted the bag over my shoulder. "Nope. I'm outta here."

Coach Theo looked incredulous. "Excuse me?"

"I'm done. I'm out." I started for the door.

"Tommy, you leave, you don't come back. You realize that."

I stared at him a long moment. "See ya," I said as I walked away.

And that was pretty much it. No big, dramatic moment. No grand epiphany. Nothing. I'd had enough, and I didn't even realize it until I was out the door.

Roscoe caught up with me, speed-waddling across the lawn like a newly freed baby rhino. "Dude, what was that all about?" he asked.

I shrugged, still unable to fully express what I was feeling.

"So that's it? You're gonna quit?"

"I guess," I replied. "Coach said if I walked, I was finished."

"Pardon my French, but that's f'd up."

"That's not French."

"You know what I mean. So, what are you gonna do?" he asked.

"What any irresponsible fifteen-year-old would do."

"Run away and join the circus?"

"No," I said, magically producing a tightly rolled joint from my jacket pocket.

"Sweet!" Roscoe exclaimed in glee. He started patting his pockets, and happiness quickly faded. "Shit, dude."

"No matches?"

He shook his head, confirming our worst fears. The closest 7-Eleven had to be a good mile away.

Roscoe fished a Swiss Army knife from his duffel bag. "Never leave home without it," he said.

"That thing has a lighter?" I asked.

"No, but it's got a magnifying glass."

I didn't follow. Sure, the joint was small, but not that small. What good would a magnifying glass do?

Roscoe plucked the joint from my hands and set it on the grass. He unfolded the magnifying glass from the knife's dense offerings and carefully positioned it in the sun. A focused sliver of white light found its target.

Moments later, the rolling paper started to smoke on its own. Roscoe kneeled down and gently blew on the smoldering joint like we were a couple of lost hikers in the mountains whose very survival depended on our ability to create fire.

Within seconds, the joint caught flame. Roscoe pinched it and raised it to his lips.

Success!

"Dude!" I exclaimed as he handed me the joint. "You're an f'n genius!"

"Agreed," he said between coughs. "And you, sir, need to work on your French."

So that's how we celebrated the end of my tennis career. If you can call it a career.

Chapter Nine

Things escalated from there—or swirled downward, depending on how you look at it. With each passing month, I fell deeper and deeper into the party scene.

Coach Theo eventually called to ask that I return to the team. I was surprised. It was a pretty big reversal. I considered his offer for a second, but decided I couldn't do it. If there was a point of no return, I was coming up on it pretty quick. Why hit the brakes now?

That chapter in my life had closed. I had less important things to tend to, like partying with my friends and getting wasted. And that was the road I went down—a journey that seemed exciting at first but would later turn into something I couldn't have predicted.

My dad noticed the change and was a little surprised that I'd quit tennis. Eventually, he confronted me, his face creased with concern. I could tell he'd been thinking about it for a while, and the words didn't come easy. "You've had a racquet in your hand since you were five, six years old," he said.

I shrugged. "Things change. People change."

"So that's why you're going to quit after all this time?"

I still didn't have the answer he wanted to hear.

"Look," he said. "I know you're smoking pot. I'm really afraid for you."

I felt bad. I really did. I never intended to let my dad down, especially after all he'd done to support me over the years.

"You're failing classes," he continued. "Your grades have dropped. You quit something you love. Twice. And what for?"

I wanted to tell him I'd pull it together, bring my grades up, find another sport. But I didn't. Instead, I remained quiet, offering no reassurance, no explanation.

"Tommy, smoking this stuff has become an issue. It's affecting you."

And that's when I launched into the teenage trial lawyer routine, stating my case before the jury—just like when I'd wanted to persuade him to let me snowboard. I told him what he wanted to hear. I rhymed off a list of things I'd do to make amends, to get my shit together.

I was good. I told him how much I appreciated all he'd done—and Mom, too. I told him I was aware of the sacrifices they had made, the hours spent supporting me in each of my pursuits. My brothers too, for that matter.

I slathered it on pretty good, making sure he knew that I knew he was a great dad. That part, at least, was true. The rest of it, not so much.

When I finally finished up my closing arguments, Dad looked at me in gentle disbelief. He had heard every word I said. But I could tell by the look on his face, he thought it was bullshit.

And he was right.

The kind of troublesome behavior I had started in middle school was developing into a pattern throughout high school. It was a dark time. I was disruptive. I was confrontational. I got into fights. I was no longer the victim, and I certainly wasn't any kind of hero.

I wound up skipping classes a lot—leaving school to get something to eat, or just going to a friend's house to play video games and get high. Before I knew it, yet another summer arrived. And suddenly I was fifteen and then sixteen years old, with an unquenchable thirst for good times.

We started to experiment with drugs, most of them taken out of parents' medicine cabinets, to get us in the door, and we loved it. I ran with the same group of friends, and we all went through it together. Charlie drank and smoked weed but, to his credit, managed to avoid the harder, crazier stuff. He was never judgmental, though. He tried the pills, and I guess they just didn't agree with him.

The painkillers were plentiful, and we came to rely on them more and more. When sophomore year rolled around, the next phase opened up.

It was a Friday night, and a bunch of us were headed over to a party at a friend of a friend's house. You know how it goes: big-ass house, parents out of town, liquor cabinet well stocked and begging to be raided.

Who could resist?

It was nothing out of the ordinary—until, by chance, I stumbled upon that eureka moment, that moment when your life is about to change and you don't even know it.

I was upstairs in search of the bathroom, in the need to unload some of the beer I'd been drinking over the past couple of hours. That's the thing about these giant houses: they might have seven or eight bathrooms, but try to find one while you're wasted. For a minute, I seriously considered pissing in one of the closets.

Navigating one of the never-ending hallways, I finally happened upon a bathroom. Opening the door, I accidentally walked in on my friends Larry and Sabine. They were hunched over the counter, doing a line of cocaine.

Larry looked up, surprised to see me. "Yo, Tommy! What's up, my man?" He was bright-eyed and cruising at some ridiculous altitude, grinning the fool's grin that comes from the sudden rush of cocaine.

Sabine was playing it just the opposite: demure, maybe even a little embarrassed. The bathroom door was still open. "C'mon, Larry," she said. "Let's get out of here. Let Tommy use the facilities."

But facilities were the last thing on my mind. I was far more interested in the fine white powder sprinkled in an uneven line on the counter.

Larry noticed my gaze. "You want some?"

"No, don't," Sabine protested. "Tommy's not—"

"Sure, he is. Tommy's a partier." Larry looked over to me for confirmation, his pupils dilated from the drugs.

Someone downstairs changed the music as if on cue. It was the Beastie Boys, "Fight for Your Right to Party."

Grooving to the music, Larry raised his voice. "Tommy's a pro. He's done this before."

A few kids in the hallway suddenly appeared interested in what I was about to do. I felt a tinge of pressure, that familiar need to belong. And what the hell? What harm could it do?

"Yeah, of course," I lied.

Sabine didn't seem to buy it, or maybe she wanted to bogart the coke for herself. Either way, I didn't care. Larry was offering, and I accepted.

So that was it—my first taste of cocaine, and my first step into the next phase of addiction. I lowered my face to the cold bathroom counter tiles and inhaled that shit right up my nose in one grand snort.

And guess what? It worked as advertised.

Minutes later, feeling rather invincible, I floated back downstairs to the party. The Beasties were still cranking it, going on about "no sleep till Brooklyn." And it was perfect, the soundtrack to the night—even the crazy guitar part.

Most sixteen-year-olds aren't capable of making good decisions on their best days. Add a healthy dose of cocaine, and those abilities plummet pretty dramatically. Any number of statistics and scientific graphs can tell you that—or you can just take it from me and my firsthand experience. By this time, bad decisions were falling from the sky and landing right in my lap.

That might explain my decision to head out with some friends to the golf course next to this ginormous house where we were, lugging along dripping-wet six-packs of Bud Light, freshly pulled from some ice bucket.

With our jeans soaking wet from the beer cans, we climbed into the parked golf carts and brought them to life. Seconds later, we were humming over the carefully groomed hills of the golf course by the light of the moon. We drank, and we drove with the accelerator pedal pressed to the floor.

Someone brought along a boom box to keep the party alive. I can't be sure, but I think it was playing that song Run-DMC and Aerosmith did together. Anyway, the music was great, and it fed our insanity. There was no stopping us.

Maybe you want to hear that this night ended in some epic turn of events, like the golf carts all crashing into the pond with my friends laughing, frolicking in the warm shallows, all slow-motion and shit.

Or that I fell in love with that rare and beautiful girl who spoke to me for the first time after a night of flirtatious glances, and after a few minutes of witty conversation, she convinced me I didn't need drugs in my life—only her.

Or some other ridiculous story twist that you only find at the happy ending of a Hollywood movie.

But no, none of that shit happened. Not at all. Sure, we tore up the greens with our reckless driving, leaving deep tread marks in our path. Sure, some kids lunged out of the carts and onto the fairways. And yeah, it was the middle of the night, and we didn't give a single shit about what kind of damage we were doing. But that was about it. Kind of anticlimactic, really, as reality often is.

Eventually, the buzz wore off and we started to return to earth. Our little adventure suddenly didn't seem so fun or even mildly amusing. Everyone just felt tired and decided to go home—a bunch of yawning and wondering why our jeans were soaking wet.

What I didn't realize was that this was the beginning of a deeper addiction, a deeper need to escape and indulge. Coke would become a part of my life for the next few chaotic, destructive years, right up until the day I walked into treatment.

So that's pretty much it—the beginning of my downfall. As some dude a whole lot wiser than me once said, "Youth is wasted on the young."

And now, with the distance and perspective of time, I can see there's truth to that.

CHAPTER TEN

TOMMY—

Fast-forward to 2012. I was twenty, twenty-one—a few years after high school and right before treatment. You could say this was the calm before the storm. Or maybe it was the storm before the calm.

Whatever it was, I was living a double life. "Double life" sounds kind of exciting, like something from a comic book: Peter Parker, timid loser and newspaper photographer by day, Spider-Man by night. Or Clark Kent, another newspaper dweeb whose nerdy glasses somehow conceal his true identity: Superman. Both of these guys lacked the courage to talk to girls in their regular life, but then they'd slip into their crime-fighting tights and kick some serious ass. I don't care who you are—that kind of story is irresistible to any teenager.

If only . . .

My double life wasn't quite as exciting, but at least I didn't have the same issues with the ladies. I was a tennis club lackey by day before transforming into my alter ego by night. True, I wasn't out on the streets fighting bad guys or saving the world. But I did become a totally different person with a totally different mission: to ingest vast amounts of drugs and alcohol, have a good time, and make enough cash to pay for my indulgences.

I was the go-to guy for my friends' drug needs, too. The problem was, I couldn't resist my own stash, and it was becoming more challenging to share it. At work the next day, at the tennis club, I would really pay for it. And when my workday was finally over, I would head out for the night and start all over again.

Now, this gig didn't exactly fall in the "strenuous" category. I wasn't even starting stupid-early like the rest of the world—just rolling in at the tender hour of 10 or even 11 a.m., the sunlight killing my eyes like I was a native of Transylvania. Most days, I was hungover. I had the dry mouth that comes from a solid night of partying, the dull hum of a world-class headache, and the desire to curl up into a fetal position and sleep for seventeen hours. Not the best of circumstances, even when you're showing up for a menial job.

In fact, I dreaded going to work so much, I had to do something just to get through the day. That something was drugs.

You know that scene in every action movie ever, with the hero preparing to leave his house and face the bad guys? It's the one where he loads the magazine in his gun, jams it home, cocks back the slide, and then tucks it in his belt—or the one where he sharpens his knife and then slips it into its sheath with that exaggerated sound effect you'll never hear in the real world. Well, that's kind of what my mornings were like, except my weapons were drugs. My demons weren't bad guys prowling the streets; they were right there in my head, and I wasn't planning to chase them away anytime soon.

Gearing up to face *my* day required some planning of a different sort.

To fight the anxiety and depression that would choke me every morning, I'd start with a little morphine sulfate appetizer: MS Contin, a not-too-distant relative to the more popular and equally delicious Oxycontin. These little bad boys came in two convenient, color-coded dosages for my consumption pleasure: 15 mg (blue) and 30 mg (purple). I always wondered if they made a 60 mg pill that glowed green in the dark like radioactive waste—something that would bury the needle of a Geiger counter. I could only imagine how popular these things would be; the purple pills were exciting enough. Double the dose, double the high—and yeah, double the risk—hitting me all at once. I'd chew that pill up, swallow it back, and enjoy the ride.

The weird part was that after taking the higher dose, the 15 mg version wasn't what you'd expect. I didn't feel high at all. Taking that first hit just brought me back to baseline, back to normal. To my normal, anyway.

Like the action movie hero, I had to prepare before I stepped out the door. So for safe measure, I'd keep a few extra pills in a discarded pill bottle I'd picked up somewhere. The label had pretty much worn off, and what was left was more or less unreadable. Preparation also involved pocketing a couple of bags of cocaine, just in case.

In case of what, you ask? In case the other stuff wore off.

That's the thing: once you go down this road, you need to maintain—maintain at all costs. Then, once your tolerance climbs, you still need to maintain, and that usually involves increasing your dose.

When your brain and judgment are already affected by drugs, that kind of rationale makes sense. Step back and look at it, and the vicious cycle is perfectly obvious. When you're in the midst of it, though, you don't have the luxury of rational thought. You're too caught up in just trying to make it through the day.

How did I become this guy? It's not like my life was so horrible that drugs were the ticket to a better one. It's not like I was raised without incredible love, opportunities, or hope for the future. Nothing like that was going on in my life. In fact, nothing was wrong—at least, nothing that I cared to think about. I had struggles in school, but perhaps that was from my lack of interest in academia on many levels. The extreme bullying at the prep school certainly had contributed to the breakdown of my morale. I was a kid who loved fun, who loved my family. But something was sorely missing.

LAURA—

While Tommy was living at home and working at the tennis club, he often kept to himself. He'd come and go as he pleased. I didn't really keep tabs on him. He was a young adult now. I needed to let him lead his own life without his mother micromanaging him. I was just happy he was working and going to school at the community college. There was little to suggest he was leading this other life.

Well, at least I didn't see it at the time.

A lot of times, I didn't really know where he was. It was a big house, and I couldn't always hear him or know exactly where he was. When I'd finally go to bed at 10 or 11 p.m., Tommy would still be there at home. I had no idea he was waiting all along for the opportunity to slip out and join his friends.

I don't consider myself naïve at all. It's not like I turned a blind eye. Whenever I saw him, he appeared normal. He didn't seem to be high. Still, I knew something wasn't right. There was something off. He was suddenly very private and unmotivated.

The only real clue was the odd pill or two that I'd find in his bedroom. I remember plucking one strange-looking purple pill from his carpet and asking him about it.

"Oh, that? Must've fallen out of my bag," he said with a dismissive shrug, as if it were no big deal to have such things lying around. "That's nothing. It's fine—just something to help with the pain from my injury." He had mangled his hand several months earlier in a motorcycle accident.

"Not fine," I said, carrying the pill to the toilet bowl for its ceremonial death by water.

I knew then that he was in trouble. Of course, I didn't realize how insane things would get. I wouldn't know the whole truth until later. But I knew he was lying to me.

Tommy was getting high yet keeping up appearances that everything was coasting along just fine. It was all part of that ability to maintain. But as in the case of most addicts, the ability to maintain as a high-functioning addict is intermittent.

Eventually, it all comes to a screeching halt.

TOMMY—

I saw a documentary on PBS once about atom bombs detonating in the desert. Apparently, you're not supposed to look directly at that shit without special glasses on. Worse than staring at a solar eclipse, they claim. Without my sweet little narcotic friends in the morning, reality was just a little too much to face.

Yet drugs were far from the most effective way to deal with the coming day. It was kind of like putting on homemade cardboard sunglasses to watch an atom bomb go off. The damage can be irreversible.

My job at the tennis club was so monotonous that I felt I had to take something. Sure, some days at the club were better than others. Teaching tennis to kids or other clients wasn't so bad. It would have been a challenge even without drugs coursing through my veins. Imagine doing it while high.

The sad part is that I barely came off as high. My body became so used to these foreign substances that it took more and more for me to actually seem like I was out of control.

With drugs, activities like vacuuming the indoor and outdoor carpet seemed tolerable. Stringing racquets was a joy. Washing windows became an adventure. Scrubbing toilet bowls . . . well, no amount of drugs could make that ugly task anything other than what it was.

On days when I worked the front desk, I'd sit there and count the minutes until my shift ended, until I could transform into my alter ego. Then night would arrive at last, and I could shed my tennis club shirt faster than Clark Kent, and dress like I was ready to have a good time. Which I was.

Buying drugs had become pretty common for me. Sometimes I'd get pills from a local dealer named Cletus, this mountain of a man who clocked in at six and a half feet tall and about 300 pounds. That's no exaggeration. He was an enormous, frightening-looking guy who could part a crowd just with the scowl on his face.

The thing was, he was a total softy.

Cletus loved his mom and talked about her all the time, in a squeaky voice that you wouldn't expect from a giant like him. He reminded me a little of Mike Tyson, another bruiser with a voice that should've come out of someone a fraction of his size. His mother had some form of cancer, so Cletus always had a good supply of meds, which certainly contributed to his undeniable popularity. All I cared about was a steady supply, and Cletus provided that.

At night, I'd ride around in my Toyota FJ Cruiser with Raymond, a buddy of mine, looking to get high. Raymond was the consummate party guy, with connections all over town. Oddly enough, he always dressed up, like he was going to some formal society function. He wore a blue blazer with gold buttons and an elaborate family crest embroidered on the chest, and he was never without a freshly pressed shirt, khakis, and a striped tie. The tie was a real head-scratcher, though more than once I did see him use it as an impromptu headband when the partying reached peak levels. Overall, this getup made him look like he'd spent the day at his father's yacht club.

I once asked him why he dressed that way.

"I dunno." He shrugged. "You can get away with a lot more shit if you dress like this instead of dressing like a criminal."

He had a point.

Dressing like a model citizen attracted less attention from other people, especially the cops. The general public tended to cut him a lot more slack even when he did behave like a raving lunatic, just because he was dressed like a sweet young man or a towering example for others. It was a ruse, and one that worked well for two young, plastered idiots out on the town.

We'd begin the night by picking stuff up and then going back to Raymond's apartment to snort some lines on his kitchen table. Then we'd hop in my FJ Cruiser—this cool-looking SUV that strongly resembles a sturdy little truck pushed around by kids in the sandbox—and I'd steer to some hopping party somewhere. In no time, we'd recklessly indulge in whatever they had to offer. When things cooled off or they ran out of drugs, I'd know it was time to move again.

I would scan the crowded party, looking for my partner in crime, until I finally found him lounging on a crowded sofa or something. I had to hand it to Raymond. He was good at being the center of attention. He typically would be pretty wasted, and unquestionably he'd be having a great time. Girls would hang on his every word, even though he often didn't make a ton of sense unless you were as messed up as he was.

When I'd shout, "Raymond!" above the din, it might take him a full three-count before he'd slowly look over, that drug daze evident in his expression. But soon he would untangle himself from some cute sorority girl and spend the next few minutes hunting for his yacht club blazer. Finding it draped over the shoulders of some other intoxicated co-ed, he would tug it away like a drunken matador.

And like that, we'd be back in the FJ Cruiser, cruising to our next stop, our next adventure. The local hip-hop station, 104.1, provided a steady beat that helped propel us forward on this errand of insanity. That vehicle would be buzzing—I'm not sure if it was the uneven road or the fact that we were both swaying to the music. Or maybe it was the drugs we'd just consumed in our friend's home. I guess it doesn't matter. We were on a mission, and nothing was going to stop us.

If we didn't have any drugs left, we would text one of the local dealers or a sympathetic friend. If I wanted painkillers, the text would read: *Any PK?*

The answer wouldn't take long: *No problem. How many?*

For cocaine, it was: *Can you share some white girl?*

A few minutes later . . . *Ding!* My iPhone would light up.

By this point, I was well conditioned. That sound triggered what's referred to in introductory psychology courses as a Pavlovian response. I knew what it meant. So I'd grin, whip the phone out, and squint at the screen through my own buzz.

Why, yes, we have a fresh shipment, bagged and reasonably priced for your convenience.

I'd respond to this all-important text while driving—dangerous, yes, but that was the least of my problems—and turn the car toward the provided address. That was the great thing about the FJ Cruiser: you could easily drive right over those little concrete dividers between lanes, and you'd barely feel it.

Although, now that I think of it, maybe that was because of the drugs.

I think they were charging around sixty dollars per gram in St. Louis back then—about enough for one person to get a buzz on. You could pour that amount onto the face of a penny without worrying about it spilling over. It came sealed in a clear plastic bag, ready for consumption.

They say practice makes perfect, and that's kind of where I landed with measuring out lines of coke while driving. Well, I wouldn't literally be driving, but sitting shotgun with Raymond at the wheel. I'd rip open the bag, untwist it, and pour out the powder, all in a few seconds while moving at seventy miles an hour with a completely blitzed driver behind the wheel. It was a special skill that, for too many years, I didn't even know I possessed.

We had our system, and it worked. Everything we needed—all the usual paraphernalia—was carefully hidden in the Toyota's glove box: our personal mobile dispensary. Balancing all this stuff on my knees became second nature. I had it down to a science, and it was a lot more rewarding than stringing tennis racquets or mopping puke off a bathroom floor.

Come hell or high water, I could handle this critical task. Nothing would deter me—not potholes or sudden stoplight changes or anything else. If you were ever pulled over by the cops, you just had to stuff everything back in the glove box and lock it, or down the front of your underwear. Thankfully, that didn't happen too often. I wouldn't recommend hiding drugs too deep on your person. That would require additional countermeasures—and that's a league that I never had to deal with, thankfully.

I heard all kinds of stories about people smuggling their drugs across international borders—sealing them up in condoms and swallowing them, or stuffing them into other body crevices that weren't used to seeing sunshine. For me, that seemed like *way* too much effort. First of all, why would you even go someplace where you couldn't buy drugs on the ground?

No, thanks.

I was only buying in small amounts, not getting huge trailer shipments from some scary cartel out of Guadalajara. This was no exotic rendezvous with an armed Spanish-speaking dude wearing mirrored sunglasses in the middle of a Mexican desert, standing next to an unregistered prop plane on a private landing strip. Nope. Our rendezvous were nothing like that. They would take place in far less thrilling locations, like the bathroom of a nearby McDonald's.

I know McDonald's doesn't have the same sex appeal as some faraway locale, and that was okay by me. Mickey D's served our needs just fine. The biggest threat to our arteries was from all those tasty fries. And since we weren't employees, we were free to ignore the little sign by the sink and not wash our hands before leaving the restroom.

A typical night would go by pretty quickly—too quickly, it seemed at the time. Our mission was simple: We wanted to put the recreation into recreational drugs. Keep it local. Keep it St. Louis. Keep it as risk-free as sharing drugs can be.

The dealers I bought from were far less dangerous than the big players out there. I didn't have to worry about broken legs, severed limbs, drive-by shootings, or kidnappings. The only real danger was that if I upset the person, there was a good chance I would get yelled at. The worst thing that might get hurt would be my feelings. And that was a risk I could live with.

I knew enough not to even think of messing with the big leagues. And that was a good thing, given the circumstances. When you're pretty baked on a daily basis, sometimes—okay, most of the time—your judgment isn't the greatest.

CHAPTER ELEVEN

LAURA—

Tommy likes to downplay danger. I think it runs in the family, like when Eddy referred to nearly severing his leg in a skiing accident as a "scrape." Both of those boys qualify as masters of understatement.

Much later, when I crawled out of the cave of denial, I found out about Tommy's trips into East St. Louis to buy drugs. People say East St. Louis is one of the most dangerous cities in America. These dealers weren't nearly as harmless as he likes to suggest. They had their business, and they needed to protect themselves from other dealers, disgruntled customers, or whatever. These guys carried guns—that much I know.

Tommy's drug pickups were something he wouldn't admit until later, after he'd gone through treatment. It definitely is one of the more terrifying parts of his story. When it's after-the-fact like that, there's nothing you can do but thank God no one was hurt.

All I ever wanted for Tommy was to be happy, believe in himself, and grasp some kind of faith. As a young boy, he had always been a sponge for information. There was no holding back on the events of his day or the open, colorful way he viewed the world. His playful, kind-spirited personality was incredibly soulful. He was so innocent! But the bullying crushed that spirit during his teenage years. From middle school through high school, he lost any semblance of truly being comfortable in his own skin—beyond the normal difficulties of any teenager. His midbrain was hijacked. As he headed toward twenty, the true demons took over and left a trail of wreckage behind them.

During this time in his life, I think he was incredibly afraid. He lied a lot. He had to cover his tracks, make up these stories in short order, and try to deliver them convincingly. He hid all of his terrible deeds remarkably well, as most addicts do. At least for a while.

There's nothing I can do about that reality now. It's part of his story and who he was; it's part of his development into who he is today. All I can say is, I'm extremely grateful that no lives were lost.

TOMMY—

It came to the point where the only thing I cared about was having a great time. And I was pretty good at it too. Does that count for something?

I did some pretty awful stuff back then. Aside from the everyday recklessness and doing drugs, I stole from my own family. Even to this day, when I think about it, I get a knot in my stomach. I hate to blame the drugs for my behavior, but I know hurting and stealing from the people I love—that isn't really me.

One incident stands out. It had to do with my grandfather, Al, who had some health problems and wasn't doing too well. We loved Al and wanted him to be closer to us. When he moved in with us, he brought a mountain of suitcases that he kept stacked in our garage.

Al was this larger-than-life character, a true eccentric. Gruff but loveable, he was a no-nonsense, old-school kind of guy. He had this gangster-like disposition, straight out of a Scorsese movie, and some say he ran up against the mob. It was easy to picture him in a different era: tailored suits, fat roll of cash, Lincoln Continental, horse racing, the occasional cigar.

And along with that gangster personality came gangster behavior. The guy's suitcases were full of treasure. And when I say *treasure*, I mean Jack Sparrow treasure: rare coins, cash, guns. Like I said, total gangster.

Having all this luggage parked in the family garage aroused my suspicions. Even if I wasn't strung out on drugs, I would've wanted to know what he was keeping in there. I just had to answer that burning question.

So one night, after everyone had gone to sleep, I decided to find out for myself.

Using a flashlight my mom kept in the kitchen for emergencies, I ventured out to the garage. The first suitcase I tried had nothing unusual in it, just a bunch of keepsakes and other stuff. I almost gave up in disappointment. But the second suitcase was a different story. After I snapped open those latches and tipped back the lid, I was greeted by hundreds of shiny gold coins.

I lifted one up to inspect in the dimming beam of the flashlight: a Krugerrand.

Krugerrands are cool-looking coins from South Africa. On one side there's some kind of deer, something you'd probably find munching grass on the African plains. On the other side of the coin is some bearded dude named Kruger—an important historical figure in South Africa, and probably no relation to Freddy from the horror movies.

Whoever he was, I wasn't in the mood for a history lesson that night. These things were worth a lot. I'd seen them in some forgotten action movie—one where the criminals all have accents and their loot is as foreign as the way they talk—so I knew the coins were straight-up legit. As I dug deeper into the suitcase, I found more and more of these weighty, gleaming coins. A few of them were silver, too.

I took a deep breath in the quiet night and contemplated my next move.

That lasted about two seconds, and then I did what any addict would do: I began to stuff my pockets with coins like I was on a sinking ship and about to catch the last lifeboat.

Tiptoeing back into the house with these Krugerrands spilling from my pockets caused more than a little noise in the dead of night. Cursing through my drug haze, I knelt to retrieve the errant coins before my mom or someone else woke up and wondered what the hell was going on.

The next day, I went to a pawn shop in St. Louis, the kind of cramped, musty place that sells musical instruments, jewelry, and whatever else desperate people can hock to pay their bills. The guy behind the counter was a little surprised to see me spill the Krugerrands onto the glass display case counter that separated us. I made up some story about inheriting them, and said I had plenty more where these came from.

The counter guy eyed me with mild skepticism. I stood there, sweating, doing my best to appear innocent. If his bullshit detector was going off, he certainly wasn't saying anything. After all, there was money to be made, especially for him. Keeping in mind that gold was at an all-time high, he inspected the first Krugerrand before nodding in approval. He didn't seem particularly bothered with details and wasn't about to ask too many questions. My kind of guy, at the time.

"These are the real deal," he said at last.

He sat down on his padded stool and, using two fingers, typed into a computer that would have been considered state-of-the-art fifteen years earlier. From some website, he read the going currency rates and scratched out a quick calculation on a legal pad (which was probably the only thing that was legal within a two-mile radius).

Then he slid a cashbox out from under the counter and peeled off a stack of fifties and hundreds. I leafed through the bills, counting my haul before pushing the wad of cash deep into the pockets of my jeans.

That was easy, I thought.

This went on for a few days: me showing up with more and more of Al's coins, the counter guy counting off my payment. We developed this super-convenient, no-questions-asked type of relationship.

Despite my drug-induced state of mind, even then I knew this was fundamentally dishonest. I knew I was stealing. I knew if Al ever found out, he would be extremely disappointed in me. Yet I still continued to do it.

This is part of the ongoing tug of war when you're an addict. Sometimes, you're aware that what you're doing is just flat-out wrong. But that doesn't mean you can help yourself from doing it.

As you're probably aware from all the movies and TV shows dealing with drug culture, the preferred and often only form of exchange is cold, hard cash. I'm not sure why they call it that, when money handed back and forth between addicts and dealers is anything but *cold*. In my experience, it was often warm, sticky, and hidden in questionable places by eager, irresponsible junkies.

And *hard*? Definitely not. These were twenties and hundies that had been folded and refolded millions of times, giving them that soft, well-used money feel. Drug cash often has been liberated from the purse or wallet of an unsuspecting parent or grandparent. So, no, the cash I exchanged in those years was definitely not cold or hard.

After I found Al's foreign coins, however, it was plentiful.

And if I had to use a single word to describe my favorite kind of cash, *plentiful* would be it. But all that cash still needed to be put somewhere. There's only so much you can deposit legitimately in a bank, all at once, before eyebrows begin to rise and questions are asked. That's the last thing I needed, especially when I was high.

My solution was to hide the money.

At first it was simple. I hid the cash around the house—coffee tins in the family garden, that kind of thing.

But as I made those trips to the pawn shop again and again, I realized that all that money needed to be parked somewhere safe. I'm not talking rooms full of the stuff, but you know: twenty, thirty, forty thousand dollars. Few people ever get to see that much cash all at once. I decided my best bet was to make a deposit in my trusty safe deposit box at our local bank.

So one Monday morning, I arrived early enough that I could still be at work on time. It was a smaller bank, not one of the nationally recognized banks, but a real bank just the same. The bank rep had me sign in, then walked me back to the vault. That first time, I wore sunglasses. I was going for that incognito, Jason Bourne feel.

Now that I think about it, an international spy likely would not wear sunglasses indoors. Aside from the nerd factor, you'd probably draw more attention to yourself, unless you happen to live in LA, where I hear that kind of d-bag behavior is fairly common. Mostly,

I wore sunglasses to hide my eyes from the sun (which is, of course, their intended purpose)—and to disguise the truth about what I'd been doing the night before. But that day, I wore them anyway.

The bank vault was dark and cool, not to mention quiet. For a moment, it made me just want to escape—lie down on the floor and have a long nap. But unfortunately, that was not an option.

After a few trips to the vault over the coming months, the bank rep was starting to get to know me. She would greet me with her winning smile and call me by name, eventually dropping the *Mr. Boldt* stuff and addressing me as *Tommy*. She wasn't much older than I was, and there was something about her I liked. She was attractive, nice, and friendly—not flirty, but respectful.

But I didn't want to risk getting too chummy with her. The last thing I needed was questions.

Who are you?

Why're you wearing sunglasses inside a bank?

Are you from LA?

What're you doing, visiting your safe deposit box on a regular basis?

In reality, we'd walk in silence down the bank corridor, the sound of her heels clicking off the shiny tile floor. She always dressed conservatively, her auburn hair in a bun—probably something in the employee rule book under the Acceptable Appearance section. Still, she looked good, and I always wondered if there was more to her.

In the vault, she'd insert the bank key while I inserted my own key. Once both keys were turned, the safe deposit box would unlock with a click.

Our eyes would meet for the briefest of moments.

"Let me know when you're finished," she'd say with a smile. And that was it. She'd turn and walk back out to her little desk to do whatever it was twenty-two-year-old bank employees did.

Chapter Eleven

Alone in the vault, the weight of my paranoia would momentarily lift. Confident that I was safe, I'd pull the box from the wall and set it down on the tabletop. If I wasn't careful, the metal container would clang off the marble surface. The acoustics in that vault were amazing, and that shit could be loud. Or maybe it was just my hangover. I guess I'll never know.

When I lifted the lid to look down on my illicit stash, there was something weirdly satisfying about gazing down at this metal box packed with money: nice, neat rows of cash, crisply ordered with paper bands. Banker's bundles. Little stacks of possibility.

New stereo? No problem.

New laptop? Why, of course.

A killer off-roading winch for my truck? Sure—just say how many.

I kept a gun in that box, too.

I'm not sure why, but there was something reassuring about having it there: a Smith & Wesson 9mm automatic, crammed in among all that hard currency. Sometimes I'd lift the gun just to feel the weight of it in my hand.

Just in case.

In case of what, I wasn't sure. But I knew it was better to be safe than sorry. Part of me wished I had all the other stuff Jason Bourne had in his safe deposit box too: multiple passports, burner phones, currency from exotic countries, Clearasil, and whatever else movie spies needed to get the girl and save the world from evil.

Except I wasn't into saving the world.

I was into saving cash.

I slipped the money out of my jacket pocket and added it to the stash in the safe deposit box, using my weight to press down on the lid and ensure a proper close. Then I hoisted the metal drawer back up to its slot on the wall, shoved it back until it clicked into place, and locked it down.

Time to head to my other life—my less exciting, brutally mind-numbing existence, where I painfully watched the clock in anticipation of the night to come.

It sucked being Peter Parker when you knew you could turn into Spider-Man.

I paused to look down on that cool, polished floor. Ten minutes, that's all I'd need. Just a quick nap before braving the day.

LAURA—

I knew about the safe deposit box, but I had no idea what Tommy had in it. There were a few suggestions that he was making a little more money than a tennis club employee might be expected to clear at the end of the month, especially when Christmas arrived. He's always been generous by nature, but he tended to overdo it a little that year.

Beats headsets were very popular, so Tommy decided to buy a pair for each of us in the family. At $200 each, that was over $1,000 right there. It seemed a little exorbitant for a kid who taught tennis and strung racquets for a living. We appreciated his generosity, but Tom and I started to question what was going on. We wondered where the money was coming from, and whether there was something he wasn't telling us about.

"I've just been careful with my spending, that's all," Tommy said.

I felt a pit in my stomach. I knew something wasn't right. But when I asked Tommy, he dismissed my concerns.

"I live at home. I eat at home. So it's easy, you know? To save money." He seemed so sincere. "And since everyone has been so great, I wanted to get you all something to show my appreciation."

I wanted to believe him. Who wouldn't? But I could tell this was just another notch on the barometer of how fucked up things were.

CHAPTER TWELVE

TOMMY—

Al was in pretty rough shape. His health was on the downturn, and Mom had her hands full with taking care of everyone. Things were pretty stressful, and we all started to argue more than usual, or at least that's the way it seemed to me.

Despite all that was going on in my whacked-out life, I was still the oldest. I felt the need to help out as much as I could, and that mainly meant me looking after "Wild Bill," as we affectionately labeled the youngest of our family.

Dad would often take Bill to school on his way to work. But if I was awake and sober enough, I would drive him to school as well as pick him up at the end of the day. When Bill and I rode together, it was always a good time. We'd have great conversations, or we'd crank the music to ridiculous levels. I got into trouble more than once for blasting the stereo—usually from a teacher or someone at the school, and usually because some parent complained.

Bill and I, we loved it. The music would announce our arrival before we got there, kind of like the helicopters in *Apocalypse Now*.

At home after school, my role shifted to making sure everyone was fed. Most nights it was just me and Wild Bill, and we'd order pizza. Other nights, I'd roll up my sleeves and show off my limited kitchen skills. I doubt anyone was on the verge of offering me my own cooking show, but when it came to feeding Bill and my brothers, I got the job done with minimal fuss and decent results. Hey, no one went hungry.

Luckily, we all liked the same kind of food. Bill's favorite dish was awesome and fell into my favorite culinary category of The Simpler, The Better. It was a delicacy not widely known outside of the greater St. Louis area, so you're going to have to take my word for it: toasted ravioli. People there love it. I mean, love it.

Toasted ravioli involves deep-frying raviolis after they've been coated with breadcrumbs. I know what you're thinking, but it's better than it sounds. For starters, you have these little pockets of deliciousness, filled with ground beef or cheese. We would smother the ravioli with tomato sauce out of a jar or even ketchup on special occasions, like me forgetting to go to the grocery store for the real sauce. Either way, Wild Bill couldn't get enough of those things.

We called him Wild Bill because he'd constantly run around the house like he was being attacked by a swarm of killer bees. When he wasn't running, he found other ways to maintain continuous movement. One of his favorites was racing his Razor scooter down the hallways and through all the rooms, mostly missing the furniture but sometimes not. Skateboards were also high on his list of preferred indoor transportation.

Let me tell you, it takes a special kind of agility to skateboard through the house at high speed. And Bill had that skill.

Outside, he'd keep that movement going, mostly favoring the Gator. We all loved that thing. It made just enough noise to be fun, and it was as maneuverable as hell: forty miles an hour in reverse, unless it was hooked up to a trailer. Wild Bill was a youthful, maniac driver, particularly adept at steering that thing around at high speed, never once tipping it over or destroying Mom's flowers. A lot of afternoons were spent whipping around the backyard with the odd visitor, dodging obstacles like trees and parked motorbikes.

Even though I was privately on a slippery slope to self-destruction, I was still able to appreciate watching my little brother blow off steam and genuinely enjoy himself. That's one of the things I loved about him most. There was a purity to him, a goodness—a desire to have a great time and make sure everyone else was having a great time too.

My mom and I butted heads at times. It was nothing out of the ordinary; most kids that age fight with their parents. We did, however, get into an unusually big argument one time when I was trashed. It wasn't long after my grandmother died. The details are a little hazy, but it was bad enough for me to tell Mom off before storming out the door. That's not like me. To this day, I wonder what it was all about.

I hastily packed a bag of underwear, T-shirts, and the usual stuff, and then I hit the road.

My mother was taken aback by me hauling a duffel bag toward the door. "Where are you going?" she asked firmly.

"I'm outta here," I snapped. "I won't be living at the house anymore."

She looked at me like she didn't believe me.

Without waiting for her to say anything else, I pushed past her and made for the door. Fifteen minutes later, I knocked on Raymond's door.

He was surprised to see me. "What's in the bag?" he asked, gesturing to the duffel over my shoulder.

"I need to stay here for a couple of days. Just till I figure things out." Then I noticed that he'd answered the door wearing a cloth wrapped around his waist. "What's with the skirt?"

"It's not a skirt," Raymond replied. "It's a sarong. Dudes in Malaysia wear them."

"Oh. You been to Malaysia?"

"No, but those guys know how to dress. And all my underwear is in the wash."

I looked at him. "You can turn underwear inside out and double the lifespan. You know that, right?"

"Come on in," he said without acknowledging my suggestion.

So I went inside and dumped my gear. Seconds later, we were getting high and I was explaining why I'd be camping out on his sofa for an undetermined period of time.

Raymond took a deep hit off his cigar-like joint and blinked as he slowly exhaled a steady stream of smoke. "At least you have a mom," he said, catching me off guard. "My mom, she passed three years ago. Lots of unfinished business there. Makes me wish I'd done things differently, ya know?"

It was my turn to be taken by surprise. For someone who was totally stoned and wearing a tropical skirt, he was making a lot of sense. I felt bad for the guy.

"Said some stuff I wish I hadn't said. Stuff I wish I could take back," he continued. "But until someone invents a time machine, I'm going to have to live with that." He nodded to himself as if resigned to the shitty hand he'd been dealt, and offered me the oversized joint. It might've been the biggest blunt I'd ever seen—probably would've made Bob Marley blush.

Raymond's place became my unofficial crash pad until I figured out my next move. That next move came a few days later with a phone call from my brother Eddy.

It was early—early for me, anyway—when my phone buzzed on the floor next to my head. I stirred awake, and the first thing I noticed was that I'd never even made it to the sofa. We'd been partying pretty hard the night before.

Some girl came out of Raymond's room wearing the sarong. At least it wasn't going to waste. She marched past me without saying anything and poured herself a glass of water from the sink.

As I sat up, I realized I had never really gone to sleep. When the phone rang, I was just starting to doze off, my bloodstream still thick with Peruvian flake—or some other cocaine masquerading as the good stuff. Whatever it was, it was doing the trick.

I finally managed to locate my phone beneath some discarded clothing and answered. "Eddy, what's up?"

"We need you to come over to Al's house," said Eddy.

I waited for him to continue with this odd request.

"Charlotte passed away," he said at last.

This got my attention. Al's wife and I were close—super close. At first my brain had trouble accepting what Eddy was telling me. Then I sat up quickly, suddenly alert, adrenaline overriding the stew of chemicals I had consumed the night before.

"What? How?"

"She shot herself."

My heart felt like it was going to seize up. "Yeah, okay," I told my brother. "I'll be right over."

LAURA—

I honestly don't remember having a big fight with Tommy. If he did leave because of a blowout, it couldn't have been for more than a night or two. I was so focused on the arrangements for Mom's memorial, driving the boys to their practices, and taking care of Al at the same time.

When Mom passed away, we hosted the same kind of celebration of life that we would eventually do for Al: a party at the Old Warson Country Club, with enlarged photos everywhere so we could be surrounded by memories of good times and a life well lived. The boys volunteered to stand in the receiving line with my sister, Blair, and me. It was the most efficient way to have everyone approach, say something, offer their condolences. It really was a great party and a sweet way to honor Mom's life.

I was so happy having Tommy there with us, as part of the family. I was relieved that he was okay.

Not many days later, life became even more chaotic. Charlotte's cousin Damien called from Al and Charlotte's house to break the news. "Charlotte is dead," he said, coldly and unemotionally.

"No . . . no," I said. "But . . . how?"

He answered with a cool, "She shot herself in the head."

Suicide? This was so incredibly upsetting—shocking, although perhaps not a total surprise. The impact on all of us made things much more intense, sad, and downright tragic.

Tom and I arrived at Al and Charlotte's house, overcome with the suffocating weight of dread, and were met by the Richmond Heights police. We immediately tracked down my stepbrothers, Walter and Chris, my stepsister Jennifer, and her husband, John. The detectives asked us all a lot of questions about Damien, as they did not trust him.

One of the detectives was a grim-faced man, a decent person with a kind but weary demeanor. Before he allowed me into the room where Charlotte had died, he wanted to tell me something: his son had killed himself with his department-issued gun.

I was stunned. It must have been a painful admission. I could tell by the emotion he fought to contain that he'd never fully recovered and probably never would. It was an extraordinary moment: a confession delivered out of genuine empathy from a complete stranger.

After a grueling, upsetting few hours, we all headed back to our house, still realizing that feeling of shock and that awful sense of knowing that we needed to tell Al. That drive felt like the most horrible eight minutes of my life.

We walked downstairs to the lower level. Al was sitting there, upright in his bed, as we all came into his room. He could tell by the looks on our faces that something was wrong.

"What happened?" he asked.

"I have some sad news," Tom said. "Charlotte took her life."

"What gun did she use?" Al asked without missing a beat. Then he slipped into the godfather role and started barking out orders.

Maybe it was some sort of defense mechanism. I knew he was also concerned that Damien was going to loot the house. Al had never been especially kind to Damien, who was a bit of a nutcase. He'd been supporting him for years, and he had grown weary of it.

"You," he said to Damien with authority. "I want the car you've been using. I want the keys right now."

Damien was surprised and more than a little hurt. "Really?"

Al's stone-faced expression said it all: he wasn't messing around.

Damien wasn't about to argue. He turned over Al's car keys and walked out of the room.

Al's next instructions were deliberate and delivered sternly to all of us. "Laura, I want you and Tom to go back to the house," he said, adamant. "Look for cash, the guns, the coins, and get them out of there. Walter, the most important thing is the will. Make sure you find it."

And that's exactly what we did. Tom and I—along with Walter, Jennifer, and Chris—went back to Al and Charlotte's house. Unfortunately, Damien tagged along too. Tommy and the boys arrived a little later to help out according to Al's wishes. We were on such a strange mission that day. Our hearts were broken. We were devastated.

Digging through Charlotte's things, I was surprised to find a paper bindle hidden away. Having lived through my own drug days, I recognized it for what it was. It contained about a gram of coke. It was obvious that no one had used any of it. And despite the sadness, a smile came to my face. It was almost amusing to unearth such an unexpected find.

Tommy's eyes lit up when he saw it. "I'll get rid of that," he said.

"Not a chance. Hand it over," I demanded.

He didn't look too thrilled. "What're you going to do with it?" he asked.

"Flush it down the toilet where it belongs."

"I can do that."

"The hell you will." I marched straight into the bathroom and sprinkled that awful powder across the surface of the toilet bowl water before giving it a good flush.

Tommy watched the coke swirl down the toilet, a pained look on his face, as if he was saying farewell to his beloved goldfish, Fred.

Going through the house gave me this bizarre feeling. I knew Al was worried about Damien stealing his guns and Charlotte's jewelry. That afternoon, we watched sadly as Damien dug through Charlotte's purse. The desperation was difficult to witness. Al had been right about that too. But when I found the shoebox of money, I was even more convinced Al had been right to send us.

I didn't realize how much Charlotte had squirreled away. Thinking nothing of it, I asked Tommy to count it. I couldn't believe how much was there: ten thousand dollars. It was a lot to have on hand.

It wasn't until later that I learned it was more like twenty.

A week or so later, that same grim-faced detective called me down to the police department. Sitting across from me, he handed me a piece of paper: Charlotte's farewell note.

I read it with shaky hands and tears in my eyes. What it said was truly horrible—incredibly ill-spirited and so dark. To my amazement, Charlotte had blamed her death on Al and me.

When I held that note in my hands, my world came to a standstill. It broke my heart, first and foremost that she had taken her own life, but also that she wrote this outrageously inaccurate note blaming us. It was deeply hurtful, and nothing could have been further from the truth. Al and I were in a state of shock.

Years later, after countless hours spent with my therapist, it became apparent that the suicide note revealed Charlotte's intent in a very ill frame of mind. The note underscored just how spiritually and emotionally destitute she was. We came to the conclusion that Charlotte was frustrated by her inability to take care of Al because of her mental illness, and her life had become completely unmanageable. It was so deeply sad.

TOMMY—

I thought it was kind of weird that Mom acted like nothing happened, like we never had a fight. She didn't bother to ask where I was staying or where I'd been. This wasn't what I was expecting at all. I don't know. Maybe she was preoccupied with Charlotte's death. I think more than anything, despite the f'd-up circumstances that brought us all together, Mom was just glad I was there.

When she found the shoebox full of cash, she handed it to me as though it was no big deal. You would've thought it was packed with paper clips instead of hundred-dollar bills. "You better count this," she said, barely taking her eyes off the overflowing closet that stood before her.

So I took the box, feeling something flush through me. I wasn't exactly sure what it was in the moment, but it felt like an opportunity had just landed in my lap.

"Uh, yeah. Sure. I'll count it." I trotted off to sit down on the bed and started counting off this endless stack of bills.

Within seconds, it occurred to me that everyone going through the house was pretty focused on their own shit. That feeling washed over me again. I wrestled with it for a minute, looking down at my hands. There were hundreds and hundreds, probably many thousands of dollars there.

Who keeps this kind of money lying around? I wondered.

It kills me to this day to admit this, but in the moment, in the grip of my addiction, I made yet another bad choice. I did the ol' *one for me, one for you* routine, pocketing every other hundie.

I know.

I know what you're thinking.

Total scumbag move, right?

After several minutes of this, I stuffed my haul deep into the pockets of my Levi's.

With everyone still busy going through Charlotte's stuff, I slinked away, outside to the Toyota FJ Cruiser.

I opened the door, doing my best to appear nonchalant. Once inside, I popped the glove box and crammed my take in there, barely able to close the lid. It has a big glove box, that Toyota FJ Cruiser. Big enough to hide ten grand or so.

I sat back in my seat, still royally buzzed, and started to dream about the ways I'd spend this unexpected windfall.

There was so much I could've done, so many worthwhile uses for this cash. I could've donated to the church . . . sent some money to those guys who save whales . . . maybe helped out with cancer research or another truly deserving cause.

But no, not this time. Not with this amount of drugs polluting my system and disrupting my basic cognitive abilities. Sure, it's fun to dream about all the good I could've done. But the old impulses had other ideas on what to do with all this unexpected money.

Less than forty seconds later, I had my answer: the Toyota. It had been good to me. Now it was my turn to reciprocate.

She looked nice in a stock kind of way—a whole lot like every other FJ Cruiser. But this one was mine, and I decided she could use a little TLC. Some six-inch lifts would look killer and give me that extra ground clearance. I wouldn't have to concern myself with bothersome details like curbs or those concrete blocks in parking lots to prevent maniacs like me from parking in more than one space.

Some big, fat off-roading tires would be nice, too. Why do anything halfway when you can commit fully? A set of big Goodyear mudders would round out the new look, give me that monster-truck-arena swagger. Maybe they'd throw in a cool baseball hat, too.

So that's pretty much what I did: spent the money quick and hard, without too much thought, on stuff I really didn't need. Seemed to be a running theme in my life.

CHAPTER THIRTEEN

LAURA—

Tommy's girlfriend, Sarah, was one of the first people to suggest that his problems were bigger than I imagined. I still remember the phone call, remember being pleased to see her name on my caller ID.

We exchanged pleasantries before she cut to the chase. It was the first time I learned that Tommy was addicted to morphine.

"Morphine?" I asked. "How's that possible?" Morphine seemed like such an antiquated drug. It made me think of a wounded soldier from Vietnam being given a shot before a surgeon amputated his leg.

"Pills," Sarah said.

I didn't even realize morphine existed in pill form. "Are they bootleg?"

"No, they're made by a pharmaceutical company."

She tried to explain, but I was having a hard time believing what I was hearing.

Had things really gotten this out of hand and dangerous? It was a profound moment of reality. My son was in more danger than I'd realized.

So I did what any curious mother would do: I googled it. After just a few keystrokes, I had confirmed everything Sarah told me.

Google became one of my many sources of information. Every time I discovered some unidentifiable pill in Tommy's room, I would google it, and there it was: a full explanation of the drug's effects, along with a list of dangers resulting from its misuse. There was nothing comforting about any of this, but at least I knew the truth. That was certainly better than not knowing.

The extent of Tommy's problem was a mind-blowing reality slap in my face. I was terrified. I knew that I needed to do something, anything. But more than that, I needed to remain in the middle of the boat with my own sobriety. So I prayed. I prayed like hell.

It was very difficult and draining to parent an addict. It was—and is—imperative that I protect my sobriety. I wanted desperately to help my son, but I knew I had to let things unfold and not try to control the outcome.

At about the same time, we were coming up on Tommy's twenty-first birthday. Tom and I had wanted to do something special, like a once-in-a-lifetime gift. Giving him presents or money is not what we had in mind. We were big on giving our kids opportunities for adventure and learning experiences. This was a great way to create awesome memories, and that was much more appealing than traditional presents. Who really needs more "stuff"?

We decided to send Tommy on a holiday. I thought perhaps this was good timing for getting him out of his drug-crazed environment. In hindsight, rehab would have been more appropriate. I naïvely thought sending him away would help him detox, give him a chance to get away from drugs and get his head clear. Maybe leaving his usual routine behind would help sober him up. I knew that drinking would be part of the experience, but it was his drug use that I was really concerned with. Surely he wouldn't even dream of trying to take opiates out of the country. Or would he?

In retrospect, I was a complete enabler. What the hell was I thinking? I knew better.

TOMMY—

Mom has always been pretty imaginative when it comes to birthday presents. That year, she really outdid herself, like she wanted to make this birthday even more special than all the others before it. I don't know where she got the idea, but she decided to send me and Sarah on a sailing trip around the British Virgin Islands.

This was an all-expenses-paid trip to the Caribbean aboard a forty-foot sailboat—a catamaran, to be exact. I was super excited for the trip, the chance to see some remote islands, enjoy some tropical weather, and party like a world-class degenerate.

While Sarah was busy gathering her travel essentials, like sunscreen, beach attire, and sailing clothes, I was scrambling to stock up on my own essentials, which fell into—you guessed it—the pharmaceutical category. It's one thing to be out in the middle of the ocean. It's another to go out there without an adequate supply of narcotics.

In the days leading up to our departure, I made my rounds, visited my guys, and made sure I had enough pills to get me through the ten-day vacation. There was no way I was going to be caught unprepared. The last thing I needed was to go through withdrawal while stranded aboard a boat at sea.

When we finally did arrive, it was everything we were told it was going to be. BVI was awesome. The weather was perfect, the beaches were amazing, and the ocean had that tropical warmth to it that you never get farther north.

The catamaran was impressive, too. It had four separate cabins for guests, and was manned by a husband-and-wife team, Captain Ron and Cynthia. She was the cook, and it was a pretty good division of responsibilities, as she knocked out some incredible gourmet meals using local ingredients.

There were two other couples on the boat with us, and everyone was there to have a good time. And when I say *good time*, I mean *good time*.

We were introduced to a local drink that was perfect for my twenty-something palate. Ironically, this drink was called a Painkiller, and it worked as well as its name would suggest.

The Painkiller is to BVI as the Hurricane is to New Orleans. It's made from Pusser's Rum, cream of coconut, pineapple juice, and orange juice. They would shake the shit out of this mix and serve it on the rocks. At the beginning of the day, the captain would shave some fresh nutmeg over each drink. By the end, we couldn't even find the nutmeg, let alone shave it.

These tasty tropical cocktails went down far too easily, and in no time everyone was completely wasted. I was already high from my secret stash of pills, so this proved to be an ideal combo—for me, at least.

Sarah was less than thrilled. She didn't like that I had a tendency to get a little sloppy while consuming such ridiculous amounts of alcohol. She wasn't even aware of the pills, at least for the first few days. I had prescribed myself a steady regimen of Xanax and morphine. The Xanax was the easier of the two to conceal, as it didn't really need to be hidden at all.

I still remember the moment Sarah found the pills in my luggage. Standing there in our cabin, she looked awesome in her bikini top, a towel tied at her waist. She wore a wide-brimmed straw hat to help shield her from the sun, and she smelled like coconuts. Not sure if it was the Painkillers or her sunscreen, but it smelled pretty great either way.

"What're these?" she asked, holding up the pill bottle from my shaving kit.

"Xanax," I said.

She looked at me in confusion, waiting for me to explain.

"For anxiety," I added.

"We're in a tropical paradise. What are you anxious about?"

My brain searched for a good explanation. After a few moments it came back with *No matches found*.

"Tommy," she said, her words dripping with disappointment.

I did my best to make excuses, which she didn't buy. It was awkward, but I was just thankful she didn't find the morphine. That stuff was way better hidden . . . and far less easy to explain.

The next day, all appeared to be forgiven. Sarah was having a great time socializing with the other couples, and we docked at one of the many islands on our itinerary. It was pretty awesome, as you might imagine: white sand beaches, palm trees swaying in the Caribbean breeze, and a smattering of outdoor bars where tourists could relax in the sun and consume cocktails to their hearts' desire.

Yessir, sign me up.

Life was good, at least for the time being. I remember excusing myself from the table and heading to the bar's restroom. Once alone, I took out the little morphine pill that I'd smuggled in for the vacation. I swallowed it back, made a detour to the bar, and ordered a beer. It wasn't very tasty, but it was cold, and that was a good thing. I'd already lost count of the number of Painkillers I'd downed in the last hour, and I wanted a beer to offer a counterbalance.

Following Captain Ron on an impromptu tour, we wound up walking around this island paradise and splashing through the warm shallows of the perfect beaches. It was tough not to be happy in such a ridiculously beautiful place. But I still found a way.

Back on the catamaran that night, anchored not far from the closest island, the wind began to pick up. We had dined on freshly baked flatbread pizza, grilled lobster with rice, and some sort of vegetable that I was too wasted to identify. But now, a light tropical storm was enough to make everyone retreat to their cabins. Everyone but me.

Despite Sarah's pleas, I decided to stay on deck with Captain Ron and experience the oncoming storm firsthand. The boat was rocking pretty good. Waves slapped against the hull and were starting to get bigger as the night grew darker.

Half an hour later, Sarah popped up from belowdecks with another attempt at convincing me to come back with her. "Why do you want to be up here, anyway?" she asked.

"It's the storm."

"We have storms back home, too, you know."

She was right, of course, but I felt the need to experience this particular storm in this particular moment.

"I'll be down in a little while," I said. I could tell by the disappointment on her face that it wasn't the answer she was looking for.

"Fine," she said in resignation, and she climbed back down the narrow set of stairs to the cabins below.

"Good woman," Captain Ron said between puffs on his cigar.

"No doubt," I said, clinking my insulated glass against his. Some of the cocktail sloshed over the side and onto the deck, but we hardly noticed.

Within minutes, the water became choppier, the waves bigger. The next wave slammed up against us and washed across the deck.

Ron howled in delight. "That's what I'm talking about!" he shouted over the mounting storm.

I grinned back in agreement. Normally, I would've puked my guts out from this kind of crazy up-and-down motion. But I was completely out of my mind from drugs and alcohol. Normal didn't apply.

I stood up from my seat, held on to the boat's rail, and raised my face to the rain, savoring the moment. The entire catamaran rose several feet before plummeting back down with a thunderous splash.

I could hear the other passengers getting excited below. And when I say excited, I mean terrified. Their shouts of concern swirled around me in the night, disembodied voices wondering if all of us were going to drown in the storm. Meanwhile, I wasn't worried at all. Drugs will do that to you.

Captain Ron seemed to bask in the violence of the storm. He didn't seem troubled at all, and this was a guy who'd sailed around the entire world more than once. It was a pretty safe bet he'd seen worse and lived through storms that would make this one seem tame in comparison. So I followed his lead.

I also accepted the bottle of Pusser's he extended to me. It tasted even better as I raised it to my lips in the downpour.

"The Royal Navy used to issue this same rum to its sailors," he said loudly, to be heard over the storm.

"No shit," I said as I wiped some of it from my chin and handed the bottle back.

Somehow I made my way back to my cabin that night. I'm not sure if it was on my own or with the help of Captain Ron. For all I knew, it could've been the Seven Dwarves who helped me.

I awoke to calmer seas but a not-so-calm girlfriend. Sarah was still pissed at me for refusing to join her the night before. I can't say I blame her. I wasn't taking her needs into consideration, and I was basically behaving like a self-centered you-know-what.

"I hope you had fun last night. You and your new friend," she sniped.

"Did you know Pusser's was rationed to British sailors all the way up to the nineteen-seventies?" I offered.

She looked at me in disbelief, like she didn't give a shit about English naval history.

"Can you believe that?" I insisted.

Without saying another word, she left the cabin to join the others on deck for breakfast. I flopped back down onto the bed to try to grab a few more hours of sleep before it was time to start all over again.

Things didn't get any better that afternoon, at least from Sarah's perspective. As for me, I was high as a satellite sending signals back to Mother Earth.

I was slathering some sunblock onto my nose, at Sarah's insistence, when Captain Ron set down his beverage and excitedly leaned over the rail of the catamaran.

"Barracuda, six o'clock!" he shouted, pointing to something moving through the clear blue waters. Everyone else hurried to the rail for a glimpse. I stood up slowly, already wasted for the day, and took a look for myself.

Sure enough, a long, silvery fish snaked through the sea, not far from the surface.

Everyone has heard of barracudas, even if it's just from that classic rock song by Heart. But the fish type of barracuda, that's something else. Indigenous to the British Virgin Islands, it's an ugly breed that can grow to a good four or five feet in length.

These things have these sinister eyes and long snouts that never fully close, so you always have a view of their snaggle fangs. When you combine these lovely features with a super-aggressive personality, you have a pretty menacing predator.

We've all heard you shouldn't drink and dive, but what we haven't heard is that you shouldn't drink and swim with excessively aggressive fish that can literally eat you.

One of the other guests whipped out his camera and snapped a few pictures. Pictures of what, I'm not sure. From where we were, you couldn't see shit.

I frowned in confusion. What good would a picture like that be when I was back home, back at my miserable job, sharing vacation shots with my uninterested coworkers? No, I needed to get a proper picture of this magnificently ugly creature.

"Where's my camera?" I said to no one in particular. I wasn't sure, but I thought I heard Sarah say, "Oh, God," under her breath.

I rummaged through my canvas tote bag until I found it: a disposable underwater camera in its clunky plastic housing. I stripped off my shirt, wiggled my feet into some flippers, and found a mask and snorkel that may not have been mine.

"What do you think you're doing?" asked Sarah.

"What's it look like?"

"It looks like you're about to make another mistake on a trip just full of them."

"I want to get a picture," I said defensively.

"Tommy, you're wasted."

"I'm fine," I insisted.

"Captain Ron says these things bite people."

I dismissed the claim with a huff of pharmaceutical courage. "I'm sure I've bitten more fish than this thing has bitten people."

"That's the drugs talking," she whispered so the others couldn't hear.

"One time, I almost ate an entire tuna at the Sushi Hut," I said to prove my point.

By now, the barracuda had disappeared under the boat. I hurried to the back of the catamaran and slowly eased myself into the water.

"Tommy, don't!" said one of the women.

"Dude, you're nuts," said her young husband. "Forget the fish. Let's have another drink."

"Tommy," said Captain Ron in his fatherly, world-weary tone. "Be careful, okay? No sudden moves."

I nodded as I fitted the dive mask over my eyes and eased back into the warm water.

Moments later, my head was just below the surface. The noise from the boat had that faraway, muffled quality to it. I could hear my own breathing as I labored to draw air into my lungs through the snorkel. I turned slowly beneath the water, peering through the blue, searching for my prize.

Then, out of nowhere, the fish appeared. It was bigger than I had imagined, probably a good five feet or so, and silvery-blue with tiger stripes and a scary-looking head that seemed prehistoric. In the diffused light, it looked strangely beautiful.

I was mesmerized. I hung there, suspended in the Caribbean current, my arms and legs treading slowly as the fish moved closer. I raised my camera and started to snap away.

The creature seemed to notice me—an oddity, a weird intruder who didn't know well enough to stay away. I held my breath as it turned closer and gracefully passed by. It was close enough to touch.

Thankfully, I kept my hands to myself.

With a final sweep of its tail, the great fish disappeared into the wild blue depths.

My adrenaline spiked through all the drugs in my system, so it's safe to say I was pretty excited—by the danger of the moment and by the fact that somehow I'd managed to avoid catastrophe.

Suddenly, I noticed my lungs ached for air.

I kicked upward, toward the boat. When I broke the surface, I spit the snorkel from my mouth and held my camera above my head as I tread water. I'm not sure what I was expecting: shouts of joy, approval, looks of awe, maybe some clapping.

Instead, everyone gazed down on me silently with this sad disbelief. I could feel it—the kind of pity you'd reserve for a mental patient who had just retrieved his Frisbee from a minefield.

Moments of clarity were rare back then, but this was one of them. I had ignored the advice of others and exposed myself to great peril. I had taken a risk that could be classified as flat-out self-destructive. Swimming with a barracuda was a metaphor for that time in my life—a metaphor for my addiction.

CHAPTER FOURTEEN

TOMMY—

I was using pretty hard, with no end in sight. Despite that rare moment of clarity in the Caribbean, I lived most days with a foolish sense of fearlessness—a feeling that I was going to live forever, no matter how many stupid risks I took. It was probably that kind of thinking that led to the motorcycle accident.

Well, that and the big-ass bag of Xanax I'd bought earlier that day.

They ought to put a warning on the label: *Not for Use in Domestic Disputes*. I remember that I got into a big argument with Sarah, but over what? That's anyone's guess. Take your pick. Whatever it was, I'm sure it was mostly my fault. Okay, entirely my fault.

It was an epic blowout, the kind where you yell at the person you love. You go for the jugular, pushing all the right buttons, getting the reaction you want. Then come the tears, and more yelling and cursing, and then maybe someone throws a Hacky Sack and knocks over a lamp that shatters like it was dropped out of an airplane. Yeah, it was that kind of blowout.

That's pretty much the script, and I was pretty much the star of that shit show. I was also pretty pissed off. I'd had enough of this shit, of Sarah getting in my face for whatever reason. All I knew was, I wanted to get out of there.

So I did what my drug-induced instincts drove me to do: I got onto my motorcycle and started it up. The bike came to life, and I revved the shit out of the engine. It made all kinds of noise as I gunned the gas and sped out of there, popping the brake, burning some rubber. Oh, the joy of youth.

I'm usually a safety-first kind of guy, but I don't recall whether I even bothered to put on my helmet. I'll go with yes, in the interest of providing proof that I had a drop of common sense in an otherwise moronic move. Without a helmet, I probably wouldn't be here to tell the tale.

Anyway, I was saddled onto this rocket, putting some distance between myself and my home . . . Sarah . . . maybe even my problems. And I opened it up, as young guys tend to do at the helm of a fast bike. I was feeling the rush from accelerating through my sleepy neighborhood like there was an APB out for my arrest.

And then it happened.

I wish I could tell you the details of the whole thing—how it played out, how I nearly died. Maybe I could even show off a little, with some cool, dramatic description of it all. But most of what I know came from my family, as I barely recall it.

All I remember is going down that hill by our house and around a sharp turn, at about fifty or so, when the rear tire slid out from under me. The insane velocity of it all carried me like a discarded puppet hurtling along the asphalt.

And then my tire hit something—a raised ornamental curb or something—and it was lights out. Stuff like that'll happen when your response times and coordination are severely limited by drugs, and you're riding a motorcycle perfectly at home on a race track.

The bike, I later learned, decided to pick a fight with a big oak tree.

The oak won.

LAURA—

God, I still remember that December day. Tommy was upstairs arguing with Sarah, with his brothers trying to stop him. It made me so tense, so sad, knowing that Tommy was so buzzed, he was losing control.

I was talking with Al, who was very ill at the time, and we heard the whole thing: Tommy and Sarah shouting, the sound of the motorcycle revving and pulling out of the driveway, Tommy tearing away.

"Oh, Jesus," Al said with dismay. "I told him to leave that god-damn motorcycle at my house."

I looked at him, confused.

"So it would be less accessible, less of a temptation," he elaborated. "Thing's dangerous, for Christ's sake."

A few minutes later, Tom came down to Al's room. "Tommy had an accident," he said.

"What?" I had that gut-tightening feeling and thought I might be sick to my stomach.

"Peter is taking him to the ER."

"Is he okay?" I was terrified Tommy was more injured than Tom let on. I knew Tom would do that. It's part of his personality. He downplays the seriousness of things, which is probably where my kids get it from.

"Yeah, he's okay," he replied. "He's banged up, but he's going to be okay. I'm going to the hospital."

All I could think about was Tommy having some kind of head injury—or worse.

"Just wait here. I'll go," Tom continued.

"What the hell are you thinking? I'm going over there with you."

Tom knew when to back down.

A neighbor's gardener had witnessed the whole incident: Tommy storming out of the house, jumping on the bike, and racing away. He even saw the crash.

Realizing the seriousness of it, the gardener ran up to the house. "Your friend!" he said in a panic, out of breath. "The one who just drove out of here. He's at the bottom of the hill. He got into an accident!"

Tom, to his credit, ran full-out the quarter of a mile or so. He arrived to find someone else already on the scene—someone who happened to be driving by and had stopped to help lift the wrecked bike off Tommy.

Meanwhile, Peter scrambled and got the car. He drove down there, shaking, only to find his brother lying unconscious. He told me later it was the most scared he'd ever been in his life. He was afraid he'd find his brother lying dead in the grass.

After Tom returned to tell us about the accident, Al had a conniption. He was angry that Tommy hadn't taken his advice, angry that he'd put himself in such danger.

The very next day, Al died.

Al had fought the good fight, and he beat unbelievable odds right up until his last breath. He was surrounded by family when he went to heaven, even Tommy—in his altered, drug-induced state.

TOMMY—

Someone from the neighborhood happened to be driving nearby and saw me wrap the bike around the oak tree. The poor guy almost went into cardiac arrest and stomped on the brakes right there in the middle of the road. Recognizing an emergency, he forgot to put his own car into park, and it almost got away from him.

As he approached with concern, I was starting to come to. The lights suddenly turned back on, but my mind still wasn't functioning as well as it should. I looked at myself, at the mess that I'd become: my jeans were totally shredded from road rash. The whole right side of my body was bloodied. My nose was bleeding, as if I'd been chasing a parked car. Blood was everywhere. It was not a comforting sight.

And this neighbor was asking me questions, although it took a minute for them to register through the shock and the drugs.

"What're you doing?" he asked.

"What do you mean?" I responded.

"Your hand! What're you doing?"

I followed his eyes to my hands, and sure enough, one of them looked like someone had taken a sledgehammer to it. It was mangled pretty bad, twisted into an impossible pretzel of broken bone and flesh. And for some reason, I was tugging on my bloody fingers.

"What're you doing?" he shrilled again.

"Oh," I said. "I'm trying to put it back together."

The guy just about went into hysterics. "No, don't touch it!" he screamed. "Just leave it."

So I followed orders and let go of my destroyed hand.

The guy calmed down and put a comforting arm around my shoulder. Then he gently guided me away from the wreck, talking about a mile a minute. But I was having trouble following him. It was like I had water in my ears.

"You need to sit down," he said.

He was right. I was pretty light-headed. There was a better-than-even chance I was going to wind up flat on my ass, whether I wanted to or not.

Peter pulled up in the Chevy Tahoe a few minutes later.

Somehow, he managed to get me into the passenger seat and clip my seatbelt into place. It struck me as funny, imagining us getting into an accident after the accident. Peter wasn't taking any chances.

So there we were, driving toward the hospital. The whole thing still felt unreal, like it was happening to some other unlucky fool instead of me. But no, it was me. And I was about to get a not-so-gentle reminder.

The drugs weakened and failed in a matter of seconds, and suddenly it was time for the pain to take over. Sure enough, it stabbed right through my buzz. And holy shit, did it hurt.

One stoplight away from the hospital, I was consumed with the worst pain of my entire life. Everything was killing me—horrible, unimaginable agony that intensified with each passing second. I started to scream as though I'd been plunged into a bubbling vat of liquid, molten misery.

"Get me to the hospital!" I screamed.

"Where the fuck do you think we're going?" Peter shouted back. His nerves were frayed already, and me writhing and howling in the passenger seat next to him didn't help.

The next thing I knew, we pulled up to the emergency room entrance. Peter almost clipped an ambulance parked out front. Some orderlies came charging out when they saw the Tahoe buck to a screeching halt.

One ER dude had a gurney, but I was already speed hobbling for the door with two other guys at my elbows to keep me from doing a face-plant on the cement. Like the rest of my life at that time, it was chaos at its finest.

Peter was there too, saying all kinds of stuff, but I couldn't hear any of it. The pain was so overwhelming, my eyes started to spill over with tears.

Suddenly, there was a magical reprieve. Everything was quiet. The hurt stopped just as quickly as it had started.

Someone from the hospital had fulfilled his or her duty, upheld the oath taken in medical school, and injected me with some kind of sedative or painkiller, or both. I didn't care which. I felt like laughing with relief. I was falling back, slow motion, into a warm tub as a trippy, psychedelic Beatles-type song played in my head.

Minutes later, I found myself squinting up at the overhead lights in the emergency room or wherever they'd taken me. I was on my back, on one of those ER metal tables. Or it might have been a gurney. Who knows? People were gathered around me, discussing my injuries as though I wasn't even there. And maybe I wasn't . . .

Then I noticed the rubber tube. My friend! It started at an inverted IV bottle and ran to a little needle carefully taped into my vein. My body welcomed that slow, steady supply of morphine like a gospel choir basking in the Sunday rays of the Lord Himself.

Hallelujah!

I might've even heard the angels singing at that point, although it could've been just the TV on the other side of a sliding curtain that did shit in terms of privacy.

Yes, the morphine did what morphine does best. Normalcy was restored—my version of normalcy, anyway.

They cut my torn clothes away with pointy doctor scissors, and wrapped me up with bandages like I was Egyptian royalty heading for a sarcophagus. Then I was ushered off for X-rays.

"Your hand is shattered," said someone in scrubs. "Most of the bones in your hand are broken."

I nodded in acknowledgment. "Which ones?" I asked.

"Which ones, what?"

"Which ones aren't broken?"

The doctor's sigh was tolerant. He probably realized that I was stoned out of my tree. He wrote something on his clipboard, then turned and walked away.

Another doctor soon came in to schedule surgery for what was left of my hand. She examined me with professional curiosity.

"How bad is it?" I asked.

She studied my disfigured hand without looking me in the eyes. "I've seen worse," she said.

"Well, I hope so. You're an emergency room doctor."

She finally gazed over at me and smiled. "You'll be okay," she said. "We'll have you playing piano again in no time."

"Awesome. I've never played piano before."

In that moment, something weird happened: I started to get really emotional.

This is one of the less desirable side effects of morphine. Who knew? It's not like morphine runs those infomercials with warnings: *Side effects may include runny nose, irritable bowels, and emotional instability . . .*

Everyone knows me as a fairly stoic kind of guy. But not that day—not in that hospital room. I started to get all weepy and sensitive, and I didn't know why. Maybe it was the morphine, or maybe it was partly the reality that I could have died. Anyway, I was crying and blubbering—in a totally manly way, of course, but crying and blubbering just the same.

"You shouldn't be alive," offered the woman who had just come through the door like she owned the place. For some reason, that made me cry even harder—that and the morphine coursing through my system.

After a few hours in the hospital, I'd seen more than a few

medical professionals. But even in my messed-up state, I could see this doctor was a big-shot at the hospital—an administrator, maybe, or the medical director or some other impressive title. She came and sat down next to me, all serious and whatnot.

"I knew your grandfather," she said in a low voice.

Perhaps she had recognized my last name on the patient chart or whatever doctors look at on those clipboards. My grandfather, Pop—one of those amazing guys who had this effortless ability to make people feel good about themselves—had been on staff at that hospital for years.

The doctor waited patiently for my sobbing to lighten. Then she said, "Tell me one reason why I shouldn't admit you to psych and hold you."

Huh?

This was not what I was expecting.

Despite the morphine, I had enough clarity to reach into my bag of tricks, where I kept all those meticulously crafted bullshit excuses I would lob out as distractions while I schemed my getaway.

"I'm done," I said emphatically.

Her eyebrows raised ever so slightly in surprise, inviting me to elaborate.

"This is it," I continued, determined to deliver an Oscar-worthy performance. "I'm finished. I won't do it again."

I even pushed the tears from my cheeks.

"You can take that to the bank. This . . . this was the last straw. Me and drugs? We're done."

I almost broke out into that old-timey song "Breaking Up Is Hard to Do," but I thought better of it.

"Your grandfather wouldn't be happy about this," the doctor said sternly.

I nodded vigorously, as if to exaggerate my blathering, emotional state. And I waited.

"Tell you what," she said at last. "I'm going to give you the benefit of the doubt."

"Thank you," I said, managing a smile through my tears. Daniel Day-Lewis had nothing on me. A lie detector wouldn't have registered even a blip.

"But if you ever come back here again, I'm going to admit you. Understand?"

"Yes, ma'am. Yes, *doctor,* ma'am. Totally. Completely. You can count on me. I'm done with that life." Addicts have a tough time knowing when to stop talking, particularly when they're high.

She looked at me a long while, the trace of skepticism on her face. Finally, she nodded and gazed down at that clipboard of hers. Then she stood up and left the room.

I had passed the audition.

That night, of course, I was right back in character, gobbling Vicodin like it was trail mix.

For a few seconds, just a few, I kind of felt guilty. I had totally lied to that kind doctor, a woman who knew my grandfather and had cut me a break. Why would I do that? I couldn't have explained it to anyone, no matter how hard I tried. And I sure as hell couldn't explain it to myself.

I'd like to think that when I looked that doctor in the eye and made all those promises, I was telling the truth—in that moment, at least. My conviction had seemed real, even for me. Maybe I meant it when I told her I was going to quit.

It wasn't the first time I'd promised someone I was going to get sober. But all those other times didn't happen right before I went off the deep end.

CHAPTER FIFTEEN

LAURA—

Being in the hospital put Tommy in a new position. For one, he was genuinely scared. And who wouldn't be? That motorcycle accident really rattled him to the core. It rattled the entire family to the core.

But more important, it gave Tommy an opening, an opportunity to realize how close he'd come to really hurting himself. It was an opportunity to send out a subtle cry for help. He resisted at first. As things worsened, though, he would come to realize it was his only real option if he wanted his life back.

He had tried before to quit drugs cold turkey. I don't know if he ran out of drugs or he truly was making a concerted effort to stop. He did mention that he was afraid, and that's why he attempted it on his own, without going to rehab or anything like that.

The side effects were very recognizable to me: stomach pain, throwing up, out-of-control anxiety. But worst of all was the pacing like a caged animal. It was painstaking to watch. Tommy was afraid, angry, and frustrated.

I was too.

The first few attempts he had made to quit were at home, after a bender. Each time lasted no more than a day or two. At that point, I didn't realize the severity of his withdrawals. I would sit, stand, talk, and walk with him. I tried holding him and encouraging him while he cried. It was awful.

This damn disease! Addiction is an obsession of the mind. Yes, I feared it . . . but it also pissed me off.

Standing by until Tommy was ready was not easy for me, or for any of us. I felt like I couldn't take much more. I feared for Tommy's life, for his sanity—and for my sanity. Our family was profoundly affected by his addiction. I was frustrated, scared, and honestly, so very tired of it all. We all were.

TOMMY—

Returning home from the hospital didn't help any. When my grandfather Al died the day after the motorcycle accident, I was a mess. When you're in total pain like that, both physical and emotional, you're vulnerable. It's hard to resist looking for a way to escape.

My escape, as you probably guessed, came through drugs.

By now, I had tried to stop taking drugs on a few occasions. The first time, I was scared as shit. I knew it was going to be really hard and I would most likely puke my brains out for days. And guess what? That's exactly what happened. Mom caught on, and she tried as hard as she could to walk me through the gruesome process, second by second. But each attempt was a total bust. I told myself I wasn't going to do it anymore. I was done with trying to get clean. And back to the pills I went.

Now, to deal with Al's passing, I did what I usually would do: loaded up and got seriously baked. Large parts of his life celebration at the country club are completely gone from my memory. That's my mom's term for it: *celebration of life*. Still, it was a pretty somber affair. How could it not be? Friends and family shared bits and pieces of it with me later, but I still can't recall most of the party. What I do remember is numbing myself to the grief.

I decided to dress in my grandfather's tails for the occasion, especially knowing that I was headed to the city's annual Veiled Prophet Ball later that night. My hand was in a big, cumbersome cast, so I cut the jacket sleeve to accommodate it. So there I was, wearing vintage tails and a white bow tie with black patent leather shoes. It was totally inappropriate for the life celebration—yet another display of questionable judgment by someone who was half out of his mind on pharmaceuticals.

Photos of Al were plastered to the walls—huge, poster-like images of the gruff, wonderful man who'd loved me so much. And the food after the celebration was impressive. I remember these bowls of soup all painstakingly arranged for the guests on a giant, linen-covered table. For some reason, I was drawn to these little white porcelain bowls of soup: vichyssoise, to be exact.

It sounds fancier than it was. Vichyssoise is basically cold, creamy potato soup that has some other stuff going on, like cut-up green scallions. Why I decided to consume six or seven servings is anybody's guess. It's just another great mystery resulting from excessive drug use. Cold potato juice in a little bowl—who could say no?

I downed half a dozen or so in less time than it takes for the drive-through at Chick-fil-A. Not long after setting that last empty bowl back down on the table, I suddenly stood up.

Sarah looked at me in alarm. "You okay?"

"Nope," I said, and I nearly tipped the table over in my desperate attempt to get away, plowing through the crowd of surprised mourners and weathering more than a few complaints.

Seconds later, I was in the toilet stall, hunched over a different type of porcelain bowl, giving back all that creamy vichyssoise. The soup tasted far better going down than it did coming back up. Those little, cut-up chives did a real number on my nostrils.

Sarah, being the amazing girlfriend that she was, helped clean me up and guide me back to the table. "It's a good thing you're wearing a white bow tie and not a black one," she said as she used a wet napkin to spot clean some of the vomit.

Not long after that, I nearly fell over in front of a bunch of concerned friends who were trying to talk to me. I was pretty messed up, juggling my grief and the drugs that had taken over my system.

Sarah took this as a cue for an early exit. "Let's get out of here," she whispered.

"It's still early," I protested.

"Tommy, come on. You've had enough."

"Enough soup, sure. But what's next? Salad?" I looked around, searching for the salad course.

"We should go," Sarah insisted in her gentle way.

I looked into her eyes. She knew what was best for me even when I didn't. Before I could resist any further, she took me by the arm and led me outside. At least one of us was thinking straight. I can only imagine the amount of further embarrassment she saved me from by insisting we leave.

I know what you're thinking: *Lucky this guy had Sarah there to take him home and tuck him into bed*. And sure, that would've been great, except that the opposite happened.

Sarah did try to get me home. She knew when enough was enough. But I was just getting warmed up. Puking my guts out and crashing into guests was me stretching to warm up for the main event.

The Veiled Prophet Ball is kind of a big deal on the St. Louis calendar of events. Essentially, it's a Southern debutante ball. And when your brain isn't firing on all cylinders, it seems like a perfectly logical place to go after you've just had the dry heaves and you can barely walk, thanks to all the drugs and alcohol you've ingested.

Addicts often try to plead the fifth: *Your honor, I have no recollection of armed robbery. Sure, I awoke with a canvas sack of sequentially numbered hundred-dollar bills and a Smith & Wesson .357 tucked into my shorts, but I have no idea if the one thing actually relates to the other.* In the case of the Veiled Prophet, I'm going to exercise that option. The truth is, as with Al's celebration, I really don't remember much—just a few random snippets of memory floating in a cloud of fog.

Sure, there was the expected drinking in a hotel room: the warm Bud Lights wrestled from their plastic six-pack rings . . . the snap of the lid, the fizz of the beer, some of it making its way to the carpet. I guzzled back beer after beer despite the looks of disapproval from the other people there to enjoy themselves. I started getting a little sloppy, even for me. Some tubby kid in glasses and rented tails helped me up off the floor and whispered, "Dude, I think you got a problem."

I was about to refute this suggestion and tell the kid to mind his own business, worry about his own shit. Except the words never made it out of my mouth. My body had other ideas.

Despite my intentions to keep going full steam ahead, my stomach had had enough. That beer was coming back up whether I liked it or not. And I did not like it—not one bit.

For the second time that day, I was hunched over the toilet, ejecting all that was wrong in my system. It was neither a pretty sight nor a quiet one. Retching like that at maximum volume will clear out a rented room pretty quickly.

I barfed so hard that someone else wound up throwing up too.

I'd heard that was possible but never witnessed it firsthand until then. So at the least the night wasn't a total loss. Yep, the glass was indeed half full, or at least the toilet was.

When it was all over, I sat down pretty hard on the tiled floor in my rumpled, stained tails. Correction: Al's rumpled, stained tails. Sarah was perched over me on the bathroom counter, studying me, wondering what the hell she was going to do with such a grand fuck-up in her life.

At the V.P., I recall a heated conversation over Kafka, international stock market indices, and other random subjects that I was entirely ill-equipped to debate. At some point—out in the parking lot, I think—I was smoking cigarettes with that same hefty guy who'd helped raise me off the floor a few hours earlier. I did eventually tell him off, but he stuck around and was nice to me anyway. To this day, I have no idea who the guy was, let alone what his name is. He was just a kind, compassionate misfit in badly fitted tails who was nice to me, even after I was a jackass.

After that comes a big, long blank in my memory that won't return no matter how hard I try. What happened during the rest of the night is anyone's guess. I suppose I could ask Sarah, but that would involve her actually taking my call. And that's not going to happen—at least not in my lifetime.

LAURA—

I had a number of friends' daughters walking in the V.P. that year. It was also the night of Al's celebration of life. We didn't have a service for him. That's not what he would have wanted. Instead we had a pleasant party with these incredible, blown-up photos of him decorating the walls and lots of amazing food.

Tommy was super buzzed at Al's life celebration. It was just after his surgery—only a few days after his accident—and he was looped, almost noodle-like. When I noticed his behavior was starting to worsen, I suggested he go home with Sarah. She had sort of assumed the role of caretaker in his life. I had my hands pretty full, dealing with the family after Al went to heaven.

Tommy ignored the suggestion the first dozen or so times, so I became a little more insistent. "Tommy."

He looked back at me as if nothing were wrong. "What?"

"You really need to go home."

"Mom, I'm totally fine."

I shook my head. "Sarah will take you back home so you can rest. You're still recuperating."

He dismissed my assessment with a wave of his hand and pantomimed some kind of snowboarding stance to demonstrate his alleged sobriety. Of course, he wasn't fooling anybody.

Sarah did take Tommy home and tried to get him to rest, but later that night I found out that they'd decided to go to the V.P. After all, he was already dressed in his tails. Tommy can be very persuasive when he wants to be.

Oh, god. Shit, I thought. *What's he going to do now?*

The next day, a good friend who was there at the V.P. reassured me that Tommy had behaved just fine.

"You mean he stood up on his own?" I asked, incredulous.

My friend laughed. "Of course. He was a perfect gentleman. So sweet."

It wasn't what I expected, but it was comforting to hear. As the mom of an addict, sometimes I had to be grateful for the small things.

I was so exhausted from all of this. I really hated this disease and its grip on our family. I needed to focus on my whole family, not just Tommy's drug-addicted calamities. But Tommy's accident didn't wake him up to reality as I hoped it would. He wasn't ready for rehab—not yet.

TOMMY—

The next day, and for a few days after, I overindulged and suffered from nasty hangovers that were, sadly, rather typical: dry mouth and early withdrawals. So I quickly administered a tried-and-true remedy of perfectly measured medication. Just what the doctor ordered . . . if your doctor happened to be Dr. Frankenstein, who had created this monster problem in the first place.

I was soon back on my feet, feeling my new normal, and just in time for Christmas.

I never did understand the thinking behind Christmas sweaters, but Sarah looked great in hers. She was rocking one with the expected colors, snowflake patterns, and all the rest of it—like a supporting character in one of those saccharine Dick Van Dyke Christmas specials that my grandmother used to watch.

There we were, on Christmas morning. I was less hungover than usual and functioning pretty well. My family was doing what families do, unwrapping gifts and having a generally good time. Eddy was next to the Christmas tree, ripping the paper off some gift from one of our uncles. Bill and Peter were providing a running commentary. Mom and Dad were just happy to have everyone together. It was one of those movie moments, and the world didn't seem like such a bad place.

Meanwhile, I was thinking about my next hit. It had been almost an hour since my last one. I snuck off as though I needed to use the bathroom, and instead rummaged through my room until I found what I was looking for.

I gulped that pill back dry, and it was kind of sitting there in the back of my throat, not doing its job. I tried to swallow it back again and again, but my mouth was dry from all the alcohol I'd consumed the night before. I needed a drink, something to wash it down. That pill was needed desperately in my stomach, where it could be absorbed into my bloodstream and work its magic.

I eyeballed the fish tank for a few seconds, seriously considering taking a deep gulp of aquarium water. The fish looked back at me, suspended there, slowly moving his fins. The fish puckered his lips the way fish do, and it looked like he was going to say something. It was almost like he could read my thoughts and was expecting me to dunk my face. There was probably enough water in there for both of us, but I still couldn't do it.

I returned to the living room with that half-baked aura that comes with the territory. I was coasting into my own reality, where nothing seemed real and logic was hard to come by. Sarah caught me staring and offered that killer smile, that smile that always said, *Everything is going to be all right.*

I smiled back. I wanted to apologize. I wanted to make up for the hell I'd put her through, but all of that was going to have to wait. I decided it was time to give her my gift.

This was a little more than a Christmas gift. This was a *I know I've been a nightmare and I want to thank you for standing by me* kind of gift. Department stores should have a whole section dedicated to those kinds of gifts. They would probably make a fortune. I know I would've been a regular customer.

Without saying anything, I turned to the heap of presents beneath the tree and dug around until I found the one I was looking for: the light blue Tiffany's box with a white silk ribbon.

My mom turned toward me just then and noticed the little Tiffany box in my hand. Her eyes widened, and not in a pleasant way. It was a distinct mix of horror and dread. Her mouth formed into one of those perfect *O*s, and in less than two seconds she said, "Tommy, no!"

Sarah recoiled, just as mortified. She shook her head, discouraging me from giving her the blue box. "No!" she added as she scooched backward on the sofa.

"Whaaaaaaat?" I said in my best drawn-out, drugged-out twang. It never occurred to me that these little blue boxes are kind of iconic and usually mean one thing.

Engagement ring.

"Tommy, don't." Sarah looked at me, pleading, trying to save me from an avalanche of embarrassment.

"It's just a present," I said as I handed over the gift.

Suddenly, it was quiet—real quiet.

Sarah unwrapped the ribbon like she was trying to diffuse a nuclear warhead on a nationally televised program in front of millions of viewers. My whole family watched in anticipation. Even Wild Bill wanted to know what the hell was going on.

Inside the box lay a silver necklace with a heart pendant. I had seen it in the Tiffany's display case and thought it was understated in its beauty, kind of like Sarah.

"You like it?" I asked.

"It's beautiful. Thank you." Her eyes welled with tears of joy or maybe relief. Take your pick.

My mother sank back in her seat, the color returning to her face. Poor Mom. She was afraid I was about to make another colossal mistake in a never-ending line of them.

Even though I was pretty wasted, I felt that pang of guilt. Usually the drugs do a pretty good job of keeping that at bay. But not this time.

I had to do something to take my life back. How long could I keep this up? How long could I expect everyone around me to clean up the mess that had become my life?

It felt like just a matter of time before something really bad happened. What price was I going to have to pay?

"Hey, butt-wipe!" Eddy jarred me back to reality. He held a present in his hand and was offering it to me. "You going to open this or what?"

I took the present without even looking at it. At first I had to force a smile. But then, looking around the room at these incredible people, the smile became real. It became one of gratitude. No matter how many times I messed up, they forgave me. No matter how many times I humiliated them or myself, they told me it would be okay.

Here I was, slowly destroying my life, and these remarkable people—my family—loved me no matter what.

CHAPTER SIXTEEN

TOMMY—

The whole family headed to Colorado for New Year's. Sarah, being an optimist, decided to join us. I still don't know why she stuck with me so long. I guess she really did love me and figured she could help save me from myself.

At our house in Beaver Creek, I tried to quit drugs cold turkey for about the third time. The timing for this attempt was mainly because of an inventory shortage. My heart wasn't really in it.

The whole detox process felt like I was scraping a chalkboard with my fingernails. I was barfing every twenty minutes. I was so out if it, I barely remember anything from the week we were there. I just know it was a living hell. Forget the mountains. Forget going snowboarding. I couldn't even handle breathing, let alone putting one foot in front of the other. I wanted drugs. I wanted to get out of the cage I was in. I wanted to die.

Hell, I tell you. It was hell on fire. And in the end, it didn't work.

LAURA—

Tommy tried to stop popping pills while we were on vacation at our house in Beaver Creek, about a week after his accident and Al's death. This time, I was fully aware of the danger involved in detox. My research sessions had introduced me to the very scary world of benzodiazepines. They are in a category of drugs so insidious, they can cause death if you attempt to quit them cold turkey.

At least I knew what I was dealing with. Tommy needed to get off this stuff, but we couldn't afford to be cavalier about it. I knew the risks. Even with a true support system and rehab, quitting was often unsuccessful. He was technically an adult, and legally I couldn't have a trained team come in the night and take him to a center in Idaho or somewhere, which can often save young people's lives. But I knew only too well how important it is that the willingness come from the addict.

I helped Tommy attempt to detox by titration, slowly reducing the amount of benzos he was taking. This seemed like an impossible process. He needed rehab professionals who could monitor him. But we stuck with it, and he started to feel less anxious and the throwing up stopped.

Tommy pleaded and pleaded with me to go back to St. Louis, but I knew that was where his dealers were. When we returned at last, Tom and I strongly suggested rehab. It appeared to be the only safe route.

Tommy was resistant to the idea. He wasn't ready. He was too afraid to go through the grueling process of detox. I knew how he felt: the awareness that you need help. But it needed to be balanced by the overwhelming fear and desperation that bring you to your knees.

"I can do this," Tommy said. "I will not use drugs again."

Maybe he meant what he said at the time, but I knew the desperation to get sober was not really there. It would take more field work for him to be ready, to reach that point of absolute awareness.

Knowing that he needed to truly want to get clean and sober left me with that huge pit in my stomach. I was so afraid, but I knew we had to wait it out in order for Tommy to be successful.

And that day finally came a few months later.

TOMMY—

This takes us back to 2012, the epic disaster of Halloween, and the realization that I needed help.

After Mom handed me that sheet of paper with the list of treatment centers, I trudged out of the family room and sat at the kitchen table to begin making calls. I called one place in Denver—Mountain Recovery.

The place was super popular with addicts and world-class fuck-ups like me, and apparently they did a hell of a business: they were booked pretty solid. But they did have an opening in five days.

Five days? What was I supposed to do for five days? Sign up for an Alaskan cruise? I hated shuffleboard.

The woman on the phone insisted that I not change my behavior until I arrived at their facility.

Huh? I didn't understand. Changing my behavior was the whole point of enrolling. I *had* to change my behavior if I was going to live to see my twenty-second birthday.

"Sir, it's imperative that you not alter your existing habits," she repeated. "Here, you will undergo a medical detox under the supervision of doctors. If you attempt this on your own . . ." Her voice trailed off. "The results could be harmful. Perhaps even fatal."

A license to party? What was I, the James Bond of addiction?

This was not what I was expecting. I was totally ready to stop the insanity, but this place was instructing me to do just the opposite. The amount of Xanax and painkillers I was using required some serious attention in a controlled environment. If I attempted to quit cold turkey, I would go into withdrawal and risk serious seizures.

So that began my five-day purgatory: five days of waiting, hoping, and guessing. And using. Did I mention drinking? Yeah, that too.

And why not? Maybe this was my last hurrah. Until I was under the strict supervision of the professionals, I'd have to be my own doctor. Just thinking about this made me anxious. But who was I to argue? These guys did this for a living. They were the experts.

To alleviate the stress, I knocked back some pills with a fifth of Hennessy. That seemed to right the ship and eased some of the anxiety of waiting.

Maintain—that's what I had to do. That's what I'd been instructed to do. *Nothing to see here. Keep moving along.*

Yes, sir. Normalcy and me had a date, and there was no way I was gonna break it. Even if that normalcy meant me being fucked up for the next five days, until I was able to receive the help I so desperately wanted and needed.

So here I was, released from the immediate pressures of cleaning up my act, on my own recognizance. Talk about the patient running the asylum.

What ever would I do?

First things first: I headed off to the liquor store to make sure I had enough to drink. There was no way I would be caught unprepared.

Humming along the aisles, pushing my cart, I was able to amass cases of beer and pull bottles from shelves without an ounce of guilt. Sure, my cart was starting to fill, and most people might find this excessive, but my mission was a noble one. My reasons were medicinal. Or so I told myself.

Back home, I sequestered myself in my bedroom, my provisions arranged carefully for easy access. I drew the blinds to block out the light and the rest of humankind.

Five days. It seemed like an eternity. I thought about all the other people in the world who had more difficult challenges, and I knew that I could get through this.

After a few solid hits of Hennessy, I started to feel better. My confidence returned, even if it was temporary. I scrolled through my phone to see who was around and maybe willing to hang out. But each name was met with a frown. I even considered calling Mark again, but I knew he'd likely send me to voice mail or respond with a dismissive text full of four-letter words. No, I didn't need that.

I had pissed off a lot of people and burned a lot of bridges.

I sat heavily on my bed and surveyed the darkened room that had become my dungeon. Outside, it was sunny and beautiful. The world carried on in its own natural way. But I was trapped inside, banished to this awful dilemma: I wanted to throw myself into treatment, but treatment wasn't quite ready for me.

Even Netflix was mocking me, with its stunning selection of substandard offerings.

Hours turned into days. Watching the clock didn't help, either. None of my old tricks seemed to be working. If patience is a virtue, I was in serious trouble.

With little choice, I dusted off the Xbox and fired up *Call of Duty*, one of the greatest time-sucks known to humankind. There's nothing like a first-person shooter game to while away some serious time. I was forced to be alert, focus on not getting my ass shot off, and maybe take out some bad dudes in the process. If you really allow yourself to get into it, it kind of feels like you're saving the world. And that's not a bad illusion, as far as illusions go.

The days crawled by. I mostly kept to myself, with the occasional foray into the real world. When Eddy happened to return from college, it was both a relief and a welcome distraction to have someone to venture out with. My last night before leaving for Denver, on our way home from getting some food, I parked the car outside a bar. Without thinking, I did a line of cocaine to juice myself up before going inside. When I came up from snorting the line, I was surprised to see Eddy sitting there, looking at me, his mouth open, incredulous.

I was so completely wasted, I'd forgotten my brother was in the passenger seat next to me.

For a moment, I was startled, like I'd just seen a ghost or something. I was about to ask him what he was doing there, but my brain managed to catch up before I could form the ridiculous question and further humiliate myself.

"Eddy," was all I could say.

"You okay?" he asked.

"Yeah," I said, and I threw open the car door. No point in dwelling on the absurdity of the situation. There were drinks to be poured, laughs to be had.

The next day would be the first day of the rest of my life.

• • •

My dad was the unfortunate one who had to wake me up. As was the case on most mornings after a night of hard drinking and using, it was a chore to drag my ass out of bed.

"Tommy, let's go," he said.

Sitting up, I was overcome with paralyzing fear. My chest began to tighten. My pulse quickened. My father was still talking, but my own heartbeat drowned him out.

What the hell was happening?

As soon as he left the room, I fumbled for some Xanax and a few painkillers. I found a mouthful of warm beer in a discarded can of Bud Light and washed the pills back with a grimace. It wasn't long before the drugs did their job, and then we were out the door.

On the taxi ride to the airport, the anxiety continued to mount. I asked if we could stop at the 7-Eleven so I could buy some cigarettes. The driver obliged and pulled in while my father waited in the car. He kept an eye on me. I could tell he was still worried. He didn't say anything, but he may have been wondering whether I was going to make a run for it.

Closing the door to the 7-Eleven bathroom, I'm not sure what was worse: the stench of stale urine or the early Christmas carols that crackled from the low-fidelity speakers. I decided it was a tie and did some more drugs to celebrate.

Feeling ready, I returned to the car so we could resume our journey. That's the thing about drugs: choose the right ones, and you feel like a prizefighter emerging from his corner at the bell.

We arrived at the airport, and my dad checked us in. The guy is a saint. His patience knew no limits, even though I tested it regularly. I made up another bullshit excuse about needing to use the bathroom, but really I wanted to be alone to down some more pills.

I was in the home stretch and had to honor the doctor's wishes—or so I told myself. Looking back on that day, I know what was really going on. The truth is, I was scared. I was tossing out all the weapons in my pathetic arsenal, desperate to make the daunting task that lay before me a little more bearable.

The flight to Denver wasn't that long, but I skulked off to the bathroom again. Locking the door, I joined the Mile-High Club, but not in the traditional or preferred sense. No, I was literally getting high at 35,000 feet.

Once we finally arrived at Mountain Recovery, I was completely fucked up, even by my own standards.

The initial check-in involved a search, and of course they found the rest of my stash. I was so guilty, I didn't even try to conceal what I was carrying. Finally rid of all drugs, I was allowed to return to the waiting room to say goodbye to my dad.

He greeted me while trying to control his emotions. I couldn't recall ever seeing him like this. The whole thing made me want to cry.

"You ready to go?" he asked.

Choked up, I nodded.

"Good. You can do this, Tommy," he insisted. "Fight. Fight hard."

I promised him I'd do it. I would make him proud. I wouldn't mess this up. This time it would be different.

The facility staff showed me to my room. I threw my stuff down on a small dresser and crashed onto the bed. Without even taking my clothes off, I passed out into a deep, deep sleep.

"See you in thirty days," Dad had said before he left the facility, hugging me tightly. Then he'd turned and stepped back through those double doors. But there was so much more I wanted to say.

LAURA—

There were so many emotions running through my head and heart. It was a mix of huge relief, sadness for what he was going through, and guilt. I love that boy so much, and I will always be thankful that

Tommy finally decided on treatment. He stopped denying his problem and made that leap toward getting the help he so desperately wanted and needed. The deal wasn't fully sealed yet, and there was no guarantee that he could turn his life around. But he was definitely moving in the right direction.

Knowing that he would be safe in rehab, I was finally going to be able to sleep at night. But at some level, I felt broken with shards of deep remorse. Tommy just wanted what most people want, which is a happy life untethered by pain and shame. How could I make up for my own flaws of addiction, and how may they have affected Tommy? How could I relieve myself of my shame?

In the program we refer to being a living "amends" in addition to making heartfelt verbal amends. Step 9 is all about making sincere apologies to those we have harmed, including ourselves. With that direction and suggestion, I found the only way to try to heal from my self-inflicted guilt was to keep being a breathing, thinking, living amends.

The result of making these heartfelt amends is proof that I am living a life of emotional sobriety, one that eventually makes up for the harm I caused. I haven't forgotten the past, but I'm living in the here and now with a healthy presence of mind. I owed this to Tommy, and for that matter I owed it to all of my boys and Tom.

Living in the solution is the only way I could relieve myself of the shame and remorse that I was feeling relative to Tommy and his addiction. I knew I was there for Tommy in the best way possible as a sober Mom doing the very best I could to carry the message of love and compassion for my son. I was so enlightened by his struggle and his courage.

Taking pause and feeling grateful for Tommy's courage was the first step.

TOMMY—

I awoke like one of those astronauts who has been in deep space for a few hundred years and then wakes up on a new planet, eager to demolish a cheeseburger or two. I still couldn't quite explain how I had arrived at such an f'd-up place. Not the rehab center—my life.

The trained professionals at Mountain Recovery gave me a high-powered sedative, the kind usually reserved for out-of-control dinosaurs in Spielberg movies. In this scenario, I suppose that was me: the velociraptor or whatever it's called—an extra-excitable reptile that tends to eat people first and ask questions later. That sedative could bring down one of these raging, two-ton creatures in about eleven seconds. You can imagine how effective it was on a semi-emaciated addict like me.

The phenobarbital and trazodone were necessary, the staff told me, to prevent my body from going into seizures because of the other toxins floating through my system. This was one of the many charming side effects of withdrawal from all the lovely stuff I'd been consuming on a daily basis: Xanax and the rest of the pharmaceuticals.

Things went on like that for three or four days—me in a darkened room, like a prisoner who's been sent to solitary for bad behavior. I didn't get as far as eating bugs to survive, but it sure felt like it.

After doing my time, serving my penance, sleeping off the toxins—however you want to look at it—they released me among the general population. This was tougher than you might guess. I was in complete war with my own instincts.

I already wanted to get the hell out of there. Everything in me was screaming, *Make a run for it! Get back to your friends, your family, your life!* I knew that was the wrong thing to do. I knew I had to listen to the tiny voice whispering underneath the screams, telling me to give this place my all. But the next few days were rough.

In my head, playing on a continuous loop as I wrestled with that very decision, was that awesome tune by The Clash, "Should I Stay or Should I Go." I was shuffling around like a newly rehabilitated zombie, slowing returning to the human race. The antiseizure meds were dropped from my regimen, and reality suddenly became a whole lot more difficult to face.

"Darling," they sang. " . . . let me know . . . "

Joe Strummer and the boys wouldn't let up. The song refused to leave my head.

All I could do was try to get through it.

My body had its own ideas, purging that shit from my system. I was a jittery mess of raw nerves, a lovely smorgasbord of emotions and physical reactions: oversensitive, sweating, cold, tired, anxious, depressed. With little choice, I buckled down and dealt with it all.

Fortunately, my appetite returned. When you're constantly high, you tend to stray from good eating habits. The food started to help. Slowly, I started to feel whole again.

Then came group therapy, which involved sitting around in a circle with a bunch of other fuck-ups as they confessed to their own sins and missteps. You hear some messed-up stuff in there. Still, there was comfort. I wasn't alone. I wasn't the only one struggling with addiction.

I listened and learned. I could start to see a way out. There was a lot of work to do, and the road ahead didn't seem entirely certain, but at least I saw it could be done.

For every step I took forward, though, I suddenly felt like I was being pulled back. That first day after group was especially tough.

And there were times when I really felt like getting high—like I needed to get high.

Autopilot kicked in. I started to scheme ways to pull this off. It was all I could think about. Even The Clash couldn't compete with those thoughts. It took everything I could muster to deny that impulse, something that's not exactly easy for an addict.

This was the wrestling match playing out on the floor mat of my brain as my body was purging from years of chemical abuse. It was not the best combo, I assure you.

Just as I was about to start climbing the walls, Spider-Man–style, one of the other patients noticed me scheming, sweating, and looking like a general disaster.

"What's up?" he said as he approached. "Tommy, right?"

"Yeah."

"You okay?"

"I'm not sure I can do this," I confessed.

He nodded, silent in his understanding.

"How long you been here?" I asked.

"Ten, fifteen days. It gets easier every day," he said helpfully. "You just got to stick it out. I thought I was gonna bolt too. Then something just happened. Things didn't seem so bad. And I stayed. Glad I did, too. I've seen what's on the other side, and that shit's not pretty."

He was right. Each day did get a little better. Even group became more interesting and less of a hassle. Along with my strength and other basic human functions, my sense of humor returned. Before I knew it, I was cracking jokes and livening up the place. The others started to joke around too. Everyone knows the cliché: *laughter is the best medicine*. But it was true.

With laughter came a sense of relief. Maybe I was going to make it. Maybe I could get over this and take my life back.

The therapy sessions helped more than I would have guessed.

Each one was different, and we'd talk about a wide range of topics, from messed-up childhoods to all that other woe-is-me stuff. The group had a field day with my prep school bullying. They were both fascinated and mortified, and treated it like this extreme case study in abnormal childhood development.

The good news is, all the talk therapy was making a difference. I even got an intro to the basics of the Twelve Step program. So, besides the actual detoxing going on in my system, I arrived at some startling realizations—stuff that sounds super obvious now but wasn't so easy to see when I was in the midst of it. Sitting there in my chair, in a group with the others, I actually let things sink in and take hold.

What exactly had I been doing with my life? What had I done with all those years that had now flown by? While it might sound like any moron could figure this out, the answers to these important questions didn't really come into focus until I was able to participate in these sessions. Suddenly, the bigger picture didn't seem so hard to see.

Aside from these revelations, I was starting to heal my body, too. I was putting weight back on because the food was so good and plentiful. We'd line up in the cafeteria for surprisingly decent chow. They offered pretty much everything you could think of: burgers, pasta, chicken, steak, pizza, you name it. Getting sober is rough on your body. Having an abundance of nutrients and carbs was helpful and sped things up.

The facility had a gym, too. I'd work out every morning, and I put on close to fifteen pounds in just thirty days. I started to fill out again, to look normal again. My strength began to come back.

Working out, attending therapy, eating well—this routine became my life for the next month. I was putting in the time, the effort, and the work to get healthy. Even my attitude started to change. I didn't mind sleeping in a shared room with another guy who was trying to clean up and get sober.

I had a couple of roommates in that time, and we stayed in contact for a while. Unfortunately, they're not sober anymore. Staying clean is hard, and sometimes it's not possible. I give them credit for trying, though.

Mountain Recovery had rules to keep us in line, but it wasn't too regimented. We could still talk with each other, but we weren't allowed outside contact for the first ten days. Again, that's tougher than it sounds. They also took away our cell phone. There were no computers, no internet—no connection to the outside world beyond TV. I thought about trying to catch some carrier pigeons, but it was too much effort. I didn't even want to deal with tying a message to their scrawny little ankles.

Instead, we had to resort to good old-fashioned conversations, sharing horror stories, or finding a quiet spot to sit and read. Lights out was at 10 p.m. sharp, no arguments.

It was a weird existence, the opposite of what I was used to, but it seemed to be working. Like everyone there, I needed structure in life after indulging in the kind of reckless behavior that led to me being there in the first place.

Then came family week, when everyone's family arrived to participate in their loved one's rehab. Family members attended group with us, to give them a better idea of what we were going through and ways they could support us in our recovery from addiction. This part of the program was also an introduction to learning about their own codependency.

Looking back on it, I can see family week was a genius idea. Sometimes it's not easy to get your family to stop micromanaging your recovery. This program gave my parents insight into the process of recovery and some tools to further define their role in the journey toward freedom from this crippling disease.

Day twenty-eight finally rolled around: two days to go. There was a light at the end of the tunnel, as they say, and it was not a Mack truck. No, this time was different.

The moment came when my parents asked me, "What're your plans going forward? Have you thought about it?"

"Yeah." I nodded. "I'm going to go home. Get a job. Get back on track. You know."

My mom asked, "Where are you going to live?"

I was a little surprised by the question. What did she mean, *Where are you going to live?* "With you guys," I replied.

Mom seemed to consider this for a minute. "That's not going to work for us, Tommy."

"What do you mean?"

"Your dad and I talked it over. We think you should do another ninety days in a recovery center somewhere. Continue to work on yourself."

Now I was more than a little surprised.

Normally, I would dig in, get combative, argue my point. But something overcame me, and that didn't happen this time. Instead of launching into lawyer mode, trying to make my case, I remained quiet and stepped away. I went for a walk on my own, just me and my thoughts.

One way to practice Buddhism involves walking Zen meditation, and maybe I was doing my own version of that. Whatever was the case, the walk cleared my head and gave me time to think. Deep down, I knew I didn't have a plan to go back home to St. Louis and work. Deep down, I knew there was still work to be done on myself. Sometimes it's hard to admit stuff like that, especially when you've been a reasonably functioning addict whose daily routine for a long time consisted of a steady diet of denial.

When I returned, my parents were ready for the old Tommy to launch into his argument. They braced, expecting the worst. Instead, I agreed with them.

"I'll go," I said.

CHAPTER SEVENTEEN

TOMMY—

"A bunch of guys here are going to a place in California," I said. "I'll go to the same spot."

My parents seemed pleased, maybe even a little relieved at my decision to stay on the journey to recovery. *Dumbfounded* might be too strong a word to describe their reaction, but they did look at me as though I had just announced I'd received a full scholarship to study modern dance at Juilliard.

"I'll stay here a couple more days, get the flights arranged," my dad said. "Then I'll go with you to California."

I wrapped things up at CeDAR and said my goodbyes. Everyone was encouraging of my decision. They wished me luck, and I set off with Dad.

When we hit the ground in LA, Dad suggested an early farewell dinner. We found a steakhouse in Newport Beach, not far from the recovery center, and sat down for a hearty meal. There was a sense of optimism at the table, and we were both hopeful that I was indeed getting my shit together and turning things around.

I had no trouble declining the waiter's suggestion for a glass of wine with my steak. In fact, it felt good. Plus, I knew that I'd have to get used to that situation if I was going to make it.

We arrived at Sea Recovery just after 6 p.m. The whole intake process went pretty smoothly. They did an assessment and asked me a bunch of questions while Dad signed some documents and arranged for payment.

I realized in the moment just how fortunate I was: the fact that my parents were so incredibly supportive, the fact that they had the means to put me in treatment in the first place. I knew a lot of other addicts didn't have this, and I was grateful that it was even an option for me.

A few minutes later, Dad and I were in that all-too-familiar situation: having to say goodbye. I could feel his compassion, but we avoided another emotional farewell, not really speaking much. Then he headed for the door, and I was shown to my room.

Sea Recovery turned out to be a converted two-story apartment complex. I was assigned to an apartment on the second level, toward the back, which I shared with three other guys. Each apartment had two bedrooms with two twin beds each. Since it was an old apartment building, we also had a kitchen and living room.

My roommate was a short, stocky guy we nicknamed Maximus, because he had a weird haircut that looked like the Russell Crowe character in *Gladiator*. Maximus clocked in at around thirty-three years of age. That hardly made him an old-timer, but he was older than the rest of us, who were mostly in our early twenties.

Together, we dove into the new program at Sea Recovery, ready to do whatever we needed to do. It was pretty intense. We're talking nonstop work. The whole day was spent filling out questionnaires, doing worksheets, setting goals, and talking about your life and your experiences. It's not like we were out in the Sahara building stone pyramids, but it was pretty exhausting nonetheless.

I found it interesting that the questions we were asked would linger in our thoughts. I'd often lie awake at night, mulling this stuff over: Where did I go wrong? What mistakes had I made? What could I have done differently? It's not every day someone can force you to look at yourself under a magnifying glass.

This approach was already starting to work for me. It pushed me to confront my past behavior and put things in perspective. It allowed me to recognize certain addictive behaviors and patterns. I didn't realize it right then, but I was building up the tools to avoid these traps in the future.

Every day we'd have four hours' worth of group therapy. That's a lot. If that wasn't enough, we also had one-on-one therapy sessions. Group was the most intense, though. We'd have to share our assignments, and whoever was running the group would call us out if there was any b.s.

In my case, there was plenty.

The therapists were like lead characters in a TV crime show where the detective is never wrong. They had this uncanny ability to detect bullshit. And the executive director of Sea Recovery, Grace, was the best of the best.

One time, she put her foot down and called me out in the middle of a group session. "So that's it? You think you can handle everything by yourself?" she asked.

"That's not what I meant," I said defensively.

"Yes, it is," she insisted. "You may not have said it outright, but you just told us that you don't need anyone's help."

Even as I started to refute her, I knew she was right. She went on to list ten incidents where I could have asked for help, but didn't. Ten. And she'd known me, what? A few days?

"I'm going to put you on sling restriction," she said.

"Sling restriction? What's that?"

Grace stood up and left the room. A few moments later, she returned with something in her hand. She tossed it to me.

At first I thought it was a jock strap, but thankfully it turned out to be an arm sling—the kind you wear when you bust your wing snowboarding.

In answer to the confusion on my face, she said, "You're going to wear that. Twenty-four hours a day, every day. From here on out, you'll only have the use of one hand."

"What about Sundays?" I asked.

"Sundays too."

"Why?"

"Because it will force you to ask for help."

"Why do I—"

She raised her hand to cut me off. "Take it off and you'll be in a world of trouble. Anything that requires two hands, you'll need to ask someone."

"You're serious?"

"Yes," she said in a tone that suggested I would be insane to mess with her.

"What if I need to . . . you know. Pull it out? Take a leak?"

A few of the guys in group found this pretty funny.

Grace, not so much. "Guess you'll have to ask someone for help, won't you?" she replied.

Suddenly, it wasn't so funny.

With little choice, I went along with this crazy scheme—only to figure out it wasn't crazy at all. After a couple of days of asking for help, I started to come to some realizations on my own. The arm sling wasn't about the physical stuff, like flossing my teeth or opening a jar of pickles. It was about the emotional stuff, the sobriety stuff, the difficult stuff. Wearing the arm sling taught me I didn't have to bear things on my own. It was okay to ask for help.

This may seem obvious or no big deal to some people. For me, it was a different story. I came from a family that prided itself on independence and getting stuff done. I have three brothers and a father who all like to take care of their own business. I have a mother who is independent as hell and not afraid to take charge. As a family, we shared a get-it-done kind of attitude.

It seemed somehow more manly to figure things out and do it on your own. Asking for help felt strange, less than acceptable—like putting mayonnaise on your french fries. What I learned was just the opposite: it's okay to ask for help. In fact, it can be a good thing.

Ninety days went by pretty fast. As I was nearing the end of my stay, I was feeling good, ready to embrace what came next. Some of the people at Sea Recovery were pushing for me to go into sober living nearby, in Newport—a version of extended care for the next six months. They wanted me to get a job in Newport and stay local. It sounded okay, but I wasn't sold on the idea.

I was ready for a new plan—a plan all my own.

This time was different. I wasn't about to get run over with bullshit, do-it-myself optimism. Nor was I going to fall back into my old ways. Not this guy. This time, there was hope in the air.

LAURA—

Tom and I weren't crazy about Tommy's main counselor, Sharon. From the moment we arrived at Sea Recovery to discuss Tommy's plan once his ninety days were finished, we had our concerns about her. She was inexperienced and very opinionated. To this day, I get angry just thinking about how her actions could have threatened Tommy's experience in recovery.

Sharon urged Tommy to remain in her care and extend his stay.

Tommy didn't want to stay, especially with this particular counselor, and Tom and I agreed. We knew Tommy was ready for the next step.

A young person's brain is not fully developed, and Tommy's midbrain was still in an addictive state. It takes a full year of hard work to retrain yourself out of the addictive mind. That requires constant support, hard work, and consistent sobriety. The recovery process starts the minute you stop drugs and alcohol, but it takes time to defog, to physically recover, and to think clearly. And then you have to deal with the trauma of addiction and what led to it, which takes many hours of counseling and, of course, years of maintenance.

In a quieter moment with my son at the rehab center, I called him by one of many nicknames that I've come up with over the years—silly little names of motherly affection that he'd answered to his entire life. When Sharon overheard this, she criticized me for addressing my son in that way. None of us appreciated her surly attitude, and I requested that she not be present at future meetings. From my perspective, Tommy's progress there was not due to any help from Sharon, but in spite of her.

In a rare move, Tom went so far as to speak out, openly suggesting that Sharon's behavior wasn't helpful. Yes, Tommy snuck out of an AA meeting and broke one of the rules by fraternizing with another young woman in treatment. But his punishment—being banned from attending future meetings—seemed questionable. How was that supposed to help him stay on track?

Despite all this, the rest of the people at Sea Recovery were amazing. I was especially overcome with admiration and gratitude as I got to know the director, Grace, and watched the way she helped Tommy. I learned so much from her. Her careful approach was really making a difference. Without a doubt, she was instrumental in helping us all with our family recovery.

Tom and I were beginning to see so much progress in Tommy's recovery, and this was not only a relief, but a gift of sobriety. Families, as they say, are only as well as the addict. So there was work for all of us to do, and now we had the support and direction to continue moving forward with those goals.

TOMMY—

My sobriety was now 120 days old and counting. While that may not sound like much, four months was a good start, especially for me. To celebrate this new clarity, this new direction, I decided to put together my own plan.

I wanted to return home to St. Louis. There was a halfway house there, where I would get my own room and commit to attending a certain number of Twelve Step meetings each week. The staff would make sure I was accountable for my own shit: chores, a job, the stuff you'd expect.

My mom knew a sober guy in the Program in St. Louis. She recommended him as a sort of mentor, a guide. So my plan started to take shape during my last days at Sea Recovery. My cell phone was still under lock and key, so I used the room phone and my phone card to make calls and line up some job interviews. The possibilities started to look good.

In therapy, one of my counselors listened intently to my plan, and I could tell he was impressed.

"So, what do you really want to do?" he asked.

"What do you mean?" I asked.

"If you could do *anything* with your life, what would it be?"

"I'd like to go to the Olympics," I answered without hesitation.

"Then do it."

I shrugged. "Yeah, well, it's not that easy to pull off."

"Why not?"

"I'd need to find a coach, a team, a place to live."

His reply was simple: "You can do that."

Looking into his eyes, I knew he was right. I started to shift my thinking and began to make my long-term plan right then and there.

Emboldened by this new direction and purpose, I started to make more calls. It really put the drain on my phone card.

My first call was to my old coach, Dave Piket. He was happy to hear from me and pleased that I wanted to return to the sport I loved. He recommended another coach, a guy who was working with the USSRT: the US Snowboarding Race Team.

When I got him on the line, he told me about a summer camp at Mount Hood, in Oregon. "You're welcome to come if you like," he said. "Give us a chance to see how you do."

I felt a sudden surge of excitement, reminiscent of the drugs I'd been fighting to keep from my system. I thanked the coach and said I'd do everything I could to be there.

But first, I had to return to St. Louis.

LAURA—

At the end of February, Tommy came home to do aftercare in St. Louis. He signed up for living in a sober house run by a former Marine. We were proud of Tommy for taking charge and making plans on his own. The halfway house was a good idea and provided the right environment while he worked through the next stages of his sobriety.

He found a job with a local moving company, but that didn't last long. His coworkers smoked pot on his first day of work. He asked them to not get high around him, as he was afraid it would show up in his system when he was tested. He hadn't come this far and worked this hard to derail everything now.

Since these guys weren't the most accommodating coworkers you could hope for, Tommy had little choice but to quit. But it didn't dampen his resolve, and he stuck with the Program. He made regular visits to our house for family dinners and stayed on schedule with his meetings. After awhile, he went to work for Tom's business, slogging it out in the warehouse as a general laborer.

When Tommy announced he wanted to return to snowboarding, we couldn't have been happier. We were pleased with his progress and his dedication to sobriety, and we were thrilled he wanted to return to something he loved so much. He did another month or so of aftercare and managed to save some money while working. Meanwhile, he made all the necessary arrangements to try out for a new team and pulled the whole thing together himself.

Not only did Tommy excel at Mount Hood, but he managed to land on a team whose key members were sober. That's right, sober. This doesn't exactly fall into the stereotypical snowboarding team culture, which is notorious for the partying. What were the chances of Tommy joining up with a group of sober athletes? His roommate from the team had ten years of sobriety under his belt, and he couldn't have been more supportive and understanding.

Everything felt like it was meant to be. As we watched Tommy and listened to his reports back to us, we felt a tremendous sense of hope. He had come so far in such a short time. He got help when he needed it, and he did the work he had to do. He stayed determined, stayed true. He made his sobriety a priority.

On top of all of this, Tommy dedicated himself to his return to competitive snowboarding. Sure, he had a solid foundation and skill set to get in the door, but the guys he was competing against had more experience, and they hadn't taken a hiatus from the sport. Despite this, Tommy once again prevailed through his hard work—and the support of his sober teammates.

From a mother's perspective, it was so heartwarming to see Tommy rediscover his passion. He had that burning flame in his eyes, and I could tell this was not a passing thing. All the necessary pieces fell into place. Call it divine intervention, luck, or whatever you want, but it felt like this was meant to be. To me, it was clearly a God thing.

TOMMY—

I arrived in Mount Hood, the tallest peak in Oregon. That's not saying much, but the mountain sure is breathtaking, and not only from the altitude. It's a beautiful place, and just being there felt good.

Camp turned out to be the best five days I'd had in a long time. We would get up super early, enjoy each other's company, and snowboard every day. We'd go up to this glacier on one side of the mountain that was just amazing. At that hour, the snow was still pretty hard from the previous night's freeze. We'd get all of our runs in early, because by the time afternoon rolled around, the snow would turn to mush again.

After being away from the sport for a while, I wasn't sure if I'd be accepted, but everyone at camp was amazing. The new coach was especially great. He challenged me, pushed me to my limits, and offered ways for me to improve. It was kind of a finishing school that took my technique to another level. The entire team was so supportive and welcoming, too. There wasn't any weirdness, no jealousy—just a healthy sense of competition with a good dose of camaraderie. That really helped put me at ease.

Camp couldn't have gone better. When it was over, the coach drove me to the airport. Once I dumped my gear at the check-in, he told me, "Tommy, I talked it over with the guys. If you'd like to join us, we'd be happy to have you next season."

I was so excited, I could barely keep it together.

Life was suddenly looking pretty good. My sobriety was steady. I was doing the work, taking nothing for granted. A guy I met out in Oregon offered to rent me a room in Steamboat Springs so I would be able to train in Colorado and get ready for next season.

When I arrived back home in St. Louis, I broke the news to my parents. To say they were happy would be an understatement. It's not every day you get a second shot at your dream. They appreciated this awakening, this passion to get back to where I'd left off with snowboarding.

"If you really want to do this," my mom said, "we'll support you. But you need to get a job for the summer."

I told her about going back to the halfway house and my plans to work and save some money. That plan went off smoothly, and before I knew it, I was back training, back in love with the sport I'd abandoned.

The year that followed was kind of amazing. I learned and grew so much, not only as an athlete but as a person. I traveled all over Canada and the United States. I spent a lot of time in Colorado, and the hard work paid off. I qualified for the National Championships at Copper Mountain. At this point in the game, I was all of twenty-two years old.

At the Nationals, I took to the slopes like never before. My dad was there, watching and helping out, doing the great things that make him a great dad. When it came my turn to compete in the giant slalom, I remember the look on his face and the big smiles of encouragement. As he watched me race, his look said, *You've got this one, Tommy*. Most important, he was there for me—not just at the race, but in the bigger picture.

When I finished the run, my time was announced. It soon became apparent I'd won the gold medal. Sharing that with my dad after all we'd been through, after all I'd put the family through, was one of the proudest moments of my life. I was glad it was relatively warm and sunny that day at Copper Mountain. If it was colder, the tears on my face might have frozen.

Not that long ago, I had been curled up in the fetal position in the dark corners of a rehab clinic, painfully confronting my demons as the drugs slowly worked their way out of my system. That's quite a contrast to standing at the podium in a national competition in one of the most beautiful landscapes in the world.

My return to snowboarding was just what I needed. I was back to where I wanted to be, only this time I had the tools to stay on track.

From then on, no matter how awesome things got, I always found a moment to take stock and appreciate where I was.

The following year, I enjoyed another great season of snowboarding, this time traveling all over the world, including to competitions in Germany, Austria, and Canada. Things continued to go well with the team, and I was riding with the best of the best.

My competitors were Olympians. That alone blew my mind. I'd grown up watching these guys on TV, and now I was competing against them. I had only dreamed to be on the same level with them one day, and now that was a reality.

Even though this was exactly what I had wanted, I started to feel a little restless.

How much of this awesomeness could I stomach? I was at the top of my game, but there were other concerns. Like most athletes at this level, I'd crashed a few times and sustained a number of injuries that go with the territory. Over the time I'd been competing, I had broken my arms and even my back. Back injuries are the worst. Landing in the hospital as an addict was very risky. I felt strong in my program and respected the suggestions by my sober tribe that I needed to give full disclosure to all medical professionals about my recovery. I declined any narcotics as a solution for my pain. At this point in my sobriety it was a matter of life and death . . . and I know it always will be. Acceptance of any narcotic is a sure way to fuck up my life. So, I profess my circumstances, and in return I am prescribed a nonnarcotic pain med. I have also arranged to be taken to any procedure by a sober friend. By and through the grace that I have been gifted, I have remained sober through and after my ER visits. I did what was suggested, and I am alive because of it.

More than a few times, I'd been diagnosed with a concussion, and that started to become a bigger concern. I did some reading, talked to some specialists, and became concerned about brain damage. Even though I was still relatively young, my body had taken a beating. The risks of permanent damage were becoming more apparent. It made me pause and think, *Do I really need to keep doing this?*

I started to ask myself a bigger question: What exactly did I want to do with my life?

I thought about it a lot and decided to call Grace. She was happy when I told her what I'd been up to.

"Yeah, I'm living the dream," I said. "But I'm starting to think there's something else I should be doing."

"Do you want a job?" she asked immediately.

I was stunned. "You mean, like, at Sea Recovery?"

"Yes. You'd be perfect," she replied. "You would be able to relate to our new patients, and they can relate to you. With what you've accomplished after treatment, they'd find you inspiring."

Suddenly, the pieces all fell into place. Without even knowing it, I'd found exactly what I was looking for: the opportunity to give back, to help other people after so many people had helped me.

Not long after that call, I was back in Newport and back at Sea Recovery—only this time, it was different. I felt a sense of purpose that I hadn't really known before on this level. The feeling was indescribable. I knew how these people felt. I understood where they were coming from. And they picked up on it, too. It was authentic.

Being able to connect with new patients made it all seem worth it. I was able to help them by sharing my experiences . . . all the struggles I'd gone through . . . the self-doubt . . . the whole thing.

Back home, people heard that I was sober and living this meaningful life. Some of my former colleagues, people I used to party with, starting reaching out to me, looking for advice. In their own way, they were having to try on the arm sling.

"Tommy, man," they would ask, "what do you think I should do?"

It felt good that they trusted me enough to ask for advice, to ask for help. They saw me as an example of what was possible. They knew that I had lived through hell and come out the other side, that I knew firsthand what they were thinking and feeling.

Although our stories and how we hit bottom can be different, one thing is true for all addicts: we have to come to a point in time where we grapple with addiction, and for some reason—whatever that reason may be for each individual—we fall to our knees, finally wanting that help.

My hopes—then and now—are that through sharing my story,

I can help. Those who really know my story might think, *If Boldt can do it, I can do it.*

And they would be right.

CHAPTER EIGHTEEN

LAURA—

After snowboarding, Tommy moved back to California. He had a bunch of roommates from rehab who were terrific guys, really sweet. They had all become close friends, and they shared dreams for their sobriety. It started out as an ideal situation where they could support one another and relate on a meaningful level, having gone through treatment together.

They say anything is possible if you want it enough, and that is so true. It was true for a lot of Tommy's friends, and it's true in any case relative to addiction. After all his hard work, suddenly there was so much optimism and hope in Tommy's life.

Sadly, one of these guys couldn't stay the course. Not long after they moved in, he relapsed and wound up doing heroin, of all things. Tommy tried his best to intervene, to step in and save his friend's life. He called the guy's parents, tried talking him off the ledge, offered to take him to detox—anything, really, to help save him from himself. But there wasn't anything Tommy could do if his buddy didn't accept the help.

Eventually, Tommy had little choice but to ask the guy to leave. They had an agreement that was etched in stone: if you fell off the wagon or brought drugs into the house, you were finished.

Tommy's friend overdosed, went back into rehab, and then came out and relapsed again. No matter how hard he tried, he couldn't stay clean and sober. Eventually, he died—another life lost, another tragic casualty of a villainous and powerful disease.

Unfortunately, this isn't uncommon. It happens more than most people realize. We weren't surprised, but we were still devastated. Tommy handled it as well as he could and continued to help others. I believe this awful incident even strengthened his resolve to be of service to people in need.

Still, it was a trying time. As a family, we were all so supportive of Tommy. His brothers wanted to be there for him. As a parent watching your son try and fail, you see the courage it takes. You witness firsthand the struggles, the uncertainty, and the little victories that fuel your child's journey. Tommy fed off the encouragement of others and kept at it, even when he was faced with tragedy. We were proud of him for taking care of himself and also finding a way to give back to those who needed it.

When Eddy graduated from college, he was asked to speak at a reception after the ceremony. Of course, our extended family made the trip to be there. We traveled in a close pack to celebrate these types of accomplishments. What we didn't know was what Eddy had prepared for his speech.

It was no secret that Eddy had always been disgusted with Tommy's addictive behavior—his drug use, his alcoholism. When they were kids, Eddy really looked up to Tommy, who was the ideal big brother for a long while until he veered off into self-destruction. Like the rest of the family, Eddy remained supportive and only wanted the best for his brother, but his patience was often tested.

So when Eddy gave his graduation speech, we were all taken by surprise. To our amazement and delight, he dedicated it to Tommy's courage and newfound sobriety.

"If my brother can do something as courageous and difficult as giving up something so gripping that was causing him harm, real harm," said Eddy, "I know I can do what I have to do to get through the difficult times in life."

We were stunned. It was such a beautiful and heartfelt acknowledgment.

"If I'm in trouble and I'm questioning myself, all I have to do is look to my brother," Eddy continued. "I look at him as an example of strength, fortitude, and overcoming what seems like it's impossible."

Of all the things he could have commented on at such a major point in his life, Eddy chose to honor his brother. We were moved to tears.

Tommy's influence and example carried over to his other brothers, too. His abuse of drugs and alcohol had an unexpectedly positive and lasting impact. It really informed their decisions through college and carried over into the way they live their lives to this day.

Billy never did drugs or drank. After the countless times he saw his brother pay the price of addiction, Billy knew all too well where that could lead.

Peter was always what I call "middle of the boat." After bearing witness to so much of his brother's struggle with drugs and alcohol, he knew it was something he'd rather avoid. He was his own person, unafraid to say no. He was confident and sure enough of himself, so when he was faced with peer pressure to try drugs, he'd respond with a cool, "Fuck you."

At the end of the day, Peter decided to walk away from any situation that involved exposure to drugs. It wasn't worth the risk. Having lived through Tommy's struggles, he knew all too well the potential dangers of such a slippery slope.

And despite his past struggles, Tommy continued to lead the way as a good example. He's what I call a Big Book thumper. He has followed the rules to a tee. He takes it seriously. He gives back. This may sound a little strange, but the only way you can keep what you have is to give it away. Give to others: that's how successful sobriety works. That's how it has worked for Tommy.

TOMMY—

When I was using and drinking and drugging, I was mad at God. I didn't think anybody should have to go through that kind of pain. Then, when I got sober, I realized that it was on me. I had been cutting my connection to a higher power.

There's a sentence in the Big Book that I like. It goes something like this: "And some of us stood up and said, who made all of this?" Once, in Denver, when I was maybe five days sober, I was looking up at the night sky. The stars that went on forever. And I thought to myself, *Somebody had to have made all of this. Somebody or something.* Then a sense of ease and comfort came over me, a relief I'd never known.

That was a turning point, an epiphany.

From that moment on, I experimented with a number of different religions. For a while, I was into Buddhism. I really liked what it was all about. Then I fell away from that and turned to my own personal spirituality. I strayed from organized religion to . . . well, disorganized religion, my own faith I created myself. I took little bits and pieces from just about everything and found my own way, my own path.

It was my own doing, not something that I wanted to push on other people, and it became important to me—my personal guiding light. To this day, almost without fail, I get on my knees every morning and pray to God. I don't mean Jesus Christ or anything like that, but something more like an all-powerful creator. I believe a higher power is someone or something who recognizes hard work and decency.

From my way of seeing things, I just don't push things anymore. It's healthier that way. I find a way to accept things. I try and say, *This is how it's going to be. And God will take care of the rest.* All I have to do is be the best guy I can be. And from there, it will all work out.

That doesn't mean life will be easy. You're always going to have your challenges, your conflicts. But there's something strangely comforting in knowing that God's not going to give you more than you can handle, that you can get through just about anything with God's help. All you have to do is put one foot in front of the other, and it will be okay.

So far, that's been the case for me. It has taken me a long way and moved me in a direction that's only positive. This path may not be for everybody, and that's okay. But for me, it offers a hopeful, all-inclusive belief that allows me to stay true and focused on living a good, authentic life.

And it's probably this very mindset that brought me to wrap up one of the remaining bits of unfinished business from my past.

Years later, stealing from Al still weighed on me. I knew I owed his family a ton of money—money that I'd stolen from Al. As part of my sobriety, I needed to reach out to those people whom I'd affected, to confess what I'd done. It sounds easy now, but it was pretty hard to pull off at the time.

I needed to make things right.

By my calculations, I took about $20,000 from those suitcases. That money was meant for Al's kids, my uncles and my aunt. We're talking about great people here, people I was close to. Family.

Chapter Eighteen

This was a very hard lesson in my path to sobriety. I had to make right all the wrongs I had done. It was even tougher because I was close to them, and it was a lot of money. But I had to do this. I had to prepare myself for the consequences and deal with it like a man.

When I finally did get up the nerve to apologize, it was a couple of years later. I was still living in California, working at a job that wasn't the most promising, but it was a job just the same. I was sitting at my desk when break time finally rolled around, and just like that, I decided it was time.

I pushed back my chair, left my cubicle, and went outside behind the office building, next to an overflowing dumpster and some abandoned boxes. That's where I made the first call.

The phone rang and rang. Just when I was sure it was heading to voice mail, my uncle Walter answered. Like always, he seemed genuinely happy to hear from me.

"Tommy! What's going on?" he asked.

"Just checking in," I said. It had been almost a year since I'd seen him or my other uncle, Chris. Both of them live in Texas, so it wasn't always easy to get together.

"How's life?" he asked.

"Oh, you know. Pretty good. Living in Newport Beach."

We exchanged that kind of small talk as I did my best to stay focused. As tempting as it was, I wasn't going to end this call without coming clean.

Finally, I made my move. "Walter," I said without any kind of smooth transition.

He paused, waiting for me to continue.

"Something I have to tell you."

He could sense my apprehension, the awkwardness of what I was about to do.

"Sure. Go ahead."

"There's some stuff that happened a few years ago," I continued. "Some stuff that I feel really bad about."

He was silent, waiting for me to elaborate. It was now or never.

"I stole from you."

"What do you mean?"

"I stole from Al's suitcases. The ones in the garage. They were full of coins."

"The Krugerrands?"

"Yeah. I know those were meant for you and Uncle Chris and Aunt Jennifer."

Walter was quiet.

I pressed on. "It's been weighing on me for a long time. I feel awful about it. Sick to my stomach. It's a lot of money, and I needed to tell you."

"That's a heavy burden for you to carry for so long," he said.

I was amazed. Yeah, he had always been cool, but this was above and beyond. He didn't seem pissed. He didn't even seem surprised.

"I want to make it right," I told him. "Tell me what you want me to do."

"You've already done it," he replied.

I wasn't sure what he meant.

"You're sober," he said. "The only thing you can do now is stay sober."

I almost couldn't believe what I was hearing.

"That's the most important thing," he said. "You do that, and everything will be fine."

After the call, I felt like a gorilla had climbed off my shoulders. I was so light-headed, I almost didn't want to return to work. I looked down at my watch. I still had enough time to call my aunt in Missouri. What the hell! I was on a roll. Maybe this wouldn't be as excruciating as I thought.

So I made the next call, and it went more or less the same. Jennifer was unbelievably understanding. She acknowledged the courage it took to confess, and admired my desire to make things right. Like her brother, she asked that I stay the course with my sobriety.

"That what's truly important," she said.

When I finally got ahold of my uncle Chris, the last to hear my apology and confession, it was the same thing. Like his brother and sister, he responded with incredible kindness, compassion, and understanding. All of them were more interested in me moving forward, learning from this, and most important, staying sober.

I can't even begin to express how grateful I was—and still am. I'm grateful for Al's kids absolving me of some messed-up shit, and for my entire family—my mom especially. Without all their love and support, I'm not sure I could have made it.

If there's one last parting nugget of wisdom I can share, it's this: getting sober is only part of the battle. Staying sober—that's the real challenge.

The biggest thing for me in maintaining my own sobriety has been keeping a tight circle of friends who know what it's like, who've gone through their own struggles and still work to stay sober. We're all pretty close. We keep in constant contact on nearly a daily basis. If I'm going through something difficult, whatever it might be, they go through it with me. It goes back to what I learned from Grace at Sea Recovery: it's okay to ask for help. You do that, and you never have to go it alone.

Once a year, I do a trip with a bunch of these guys. We all get together somewhere for a weekend and talk about being sober.

We're like a sober network, which might sound kind of strange if you haven't experienced it. It really works.

This group of guys—my network—share their own challenges. How they deal with stuff. How they overcome whatever shit life throws at them and remain sober. How they learn, grow, and give back.

Giving back is a big part of it. Sure, you're working on yourself and ways to constantly improve, but there's something deeply satisfying in being of service to someone who really needs it. When someone is going through their own struggle, they can relate to you because you've been there. You're the real deal, straight-up legit—not some doctor or therapist.

And giving, in turn, helps you on your own path. It makes you constantly try to be better than you were the day before. As the guys in my network taught me, you really can't coast in sobriety. It's something you need to work at.

And guess what? They're right.

LAURA—

Confessing and making amends can be so scary and difficult, but Tommy did it and continues to as things rear their head. He has learned so many valuable lessons—some of life's many ugly lessons—and it contributed so much to his amazing growth and to the incredible man he is today. It is an example of his complete honesty and of maintaining his emotional sobriety.

Kids become addicts for a number of reasons, but most often we parents blame ourselves. It's easy to do. Addiction is every parent's worst nightmare. Our instinct is to think it's some fundamental failure of our own. But addiction is a disease, not a parenting malfunction. It is a disease and demise without borders.

Beating this disease and staying sober requires work. For me, that means participating in continuing education as well as working with addicts. I have been certified to teach classes that certify other sober coaches. Everything that I am learning teaches me more about myself and opens up a whole world of understanding of others. There's an incredible amount of support out there, and there are plenty of opportunities to give back. Not everyone is aware of that. But more often than not, those who truly need us, find us. Working with other alcoholics and addicts in need helps those of us in recovery to stay close to our own program. I have seen it in action. It's amazing how that works.

My first language is not sobriety. My first language is addiction. In order to maintain my sobriety, I need to work on it all the time, to learn and speak this new language.

It's important for me in my sobriety and in my life to embrace life for all it has to offer. As a family, we're active and athletically inclined, and the outdoors is a big part of our lives. We find it's healthy to focus on our passions, like snowboarding, skiing, surfing, hiking, working out, or whatever it is that makes us feel connected. These kinds of activities are vital to our emotional growth and have been huge in recovery for both Tommy and me.

Tommy and I are survivors, and we do what we need to get through life's challenges. Protecting our individual sobriety comes first. Life can be so cruel, but in every heartache are opportunities for healing and growth as long as we stay sober. We have survived what seemed like internally and externally grueling and painful warfare.

For someone like me who takes good care of myself physically, emotionally, and spiritually, while only in my midfifties, I suffered two asymptomatic heart attacks that seemed shocking but were a piece of cake compared to my active addiction. Plain and simple:

life happens for better or worse, and most often we are blindsided by things we cannot control. This is where acceptance is critical in my life. Through turbulent times I need to, as my father-in-law so brilliantly said, "Don't just do something, stand there." Tommy has a lot of the same traits as his grandfather Pop. Both are gentle, kind, thoughtful, and spiritually connected. I am so incredibly proud of Tommy's courage and strength. I admire his fortitude and commitment. I am eternally grateful for our mutual journeys.

LAURA—

My conclusion is that I also think addiction is the work of the devil. It makes people do and say things they wouldn't normally do and say. As I have seen, and as many people have experienced, the outcome can be extremely damaging—physically, spiritually, and emotionally. I know it was for me.

Oftentimes, and way too often, addiction is fatal. I believe that is why many people, like me, need faith to get through the experience and through life itself. Faith comes in many forms, with many names, but a belief in a higher power—whatever that means for each individual—is really what I need, what I want, and what I continue to lean into today.

Sometimes it is much harder than it sounds. Like a lot of addicts, I have doubted God. I have questioned His very existence: *If He does exist, how could He let me down? How could He allow these bad things to happen to me and around me and in the world?* The proof, for me, is in the action of believing.

I am learning my own way of prayer, of asking for help and talking with the God of my understanding. I'm learning to listen, to take a daily inventory, and to admit my mistakes. And I am constantly learning to welcome and absorb wholeheartedly my forgiveness of others and of myself, which is huge. This is what provides me with hope, comfort, strength, and a direction I never could have imagined prior to sobriety.

I also work on my program of recovery by waking up clear-headed every morning, one day at a time, with gratitude. I believe in working the Twelve Steps of AA and surrounding myself with healthy people. I try to stay close to my program, as if my life depends on it. And it does.

It is vital for me to work with other alcoholics in need and to participate in community service. I work hard and I play hard. I can't say enough about laughter—true laughter, not ignited by my abuse of alcohol. I love being with my husband and my boys, my extended family, and my true friends. I look forward to meeting new people, being of service to others, experiencing life and adventure, and enjoying opportunities like writing this book with my son Tommy. I embrace my sobriety. For me, this is a path to a good and meaningful life with a chance for peace.

I am a work in progress.

• • •

"And then it happens . . . one day you wake up, and you're in this place where everything feels right. Your heart is calm. Your soul is lit. Your thoughts are positive. Your vision is clear. You're at peace, at peace with where you've been, at peace with what you've been through, and at peace with where you are headed."

—Steve Maraboli

ABOUT THE AUTHORS

Laura Cook Boldt was born and reared in St. Louis, Missouri, and is the daughter of the late Mary Margaret Blair and Howard Winston Cook, both from Jefferson City, Missouri. Married to Tom for thirty-plus years, mother of four grown boys, and sister to a mix of five siblings all currently living in the US, she graduated from Colorado College with a BA in English and continued on to Parsons School of Design in NYC. Laura has also completed courses at Pratt Institute and Washington University. Currently a retired designer, Laura continues to travel, spending most of her time in the mountains of Colorado and with her family. *Unraveled*, a memoir, is her first book, and she has begun writing another non-fiction book, *Bastard by Dawn*.

Thomas Henry Boldt was born and raised in St. Louis, Missouri. He is the son of Laura and Tom Boldt and the eldest of his three brothers. He has traveled extensively across many continents for racing, surfing, and exploring. Tom remains close with his brothers and extended family. His current interests include travel, hiking, and snowboarding wherever he can, and he loves anything involving recreation on the water. He is currently living in Orange County, California, and owns and operates a small company nearby. *Unraveled* is Tom's first book.